# Union Power

# Working Canadians: Books from the CCLH

*Series editors: Alvin Finkel and Greg Kealey*

The Canadian Committee on Labour History is Canada's organization of historians and other scholars interested in the study of the lives and struggles of working people throughout Canada's past. Since 1976, the CCLH has published *Labour/Le travail,* Canada's pre-eminent scholarly journal of labour studies. It also publishes books, now in conjunction with AU Press, that focus on the history of Canada's working people and their organizations. The emphasis in this series is on materials that are accessible to labour audiences as well as university audiences rather than simply on scholarly studies in the labour area. This includes documentary collections, oral histories, autobiographies, biographies, and provincial and local labour movement histories with a popular bent.

SERIES TITLES

*Champagne and Meatballs: Adventures of a Canadian Communist*
Bert Whyte, edited and with an introduction by Larry Hannant

*Working People in Alberta: A History*
Alvin Finkel with contributions by Jason Foster, Winston Gereluk, Jennifer Kelly and Dan Cui, James Muir, Joan Schiebelbein, Jim Selby, and Eric Strikwerda

*Union Power: Solidarity and Struggle in Niagara*
Carmela Patrias and Larry Savage

Solidarity and Struggle in Niagara

# UNION
# POWER

**Carmela Patrias** + **Larry Savage**

**AU** PRESS

Published by AU Press, Athabasca University
1200, 10011 – 109 Street, Edmonton, AB T5J 3S8

ISBN 978-1-926836-78-2 (print) 978-1-926836-79-9 (PDF) 978-1-926836-80-5 (epub)
A volume in Working Canadians: Books from the CCLH
ISSN 1925-1831 (print) 1925-184X (digital)

Cover and interior design by Natalie Olsen, Kisscut Design.
Cover images: (front) Crib work construction for the Toronto Power Generating Station, September 3, 1903. D417580. Courtesy of Niagara Falls (Ontario) Public Library. (back) Hermann Sigurdsson / Shutterstock.com.
Printed and bound in Canada by Marquis Book Printers.

*Library and Archives Canada Cataloguing in Publication*

Patrias, Carmela, 1950–
Union power : solidarity and struggle in Niagara /
Carmela Patrias and Larry Savage.

(Working Canadians, books from the CCLH, 1925-1831 ; v. 3)
Co-published by: CCLH.
Includes bibliographical references.
Also issued in electronic format.
ISBN 978-1-926836-78-2

1. Labor movement — Ontario — Niagara Peninsula — History.
2. Labor unions — Ontario — Niagara Peninsula — History. I. Savage, Larry, 1977– II. Title. III. Series: Working Canadians (Edmonton, Alta.) ; 3

HD6529.N52P38 2012      331.8809713'38      C2012-901702-7

We acknowledge the financial support of the Government of Canada through the Canada Book Fund (CBF) for our publishing activities.

Canada Council    Conseil des Arts
for the Arts    du Canada

Assistance provided by the Government of Alberta, Alberta Multimedia Development Fund.

**Government
of Alberta** ■

 **Canadian Committee on Labour History**

# Contents

# Acknowledgements

This book owes a great deal to a number of people. First and foremost, we are indebted to Ruth Frager, Wayne Thorpe, and Michelle Webber, for reading the manuscript and offering helpful suggestions for improvement, and to Hugo Chesshire, Roger Fast, and Bradley Walchuk, for their excellent research assistance.

Pamela MacFarland Holway and Megan Hall, at Athabasca University Press, were a pleasure to work with, and we are grateful as well to copy editor and indexer Jon Eben Field.

We would also like to acknowledge David Sharron and Edie Williams, in Special Collections at Brock University Library, Sandra Enskat, in Special Collections at the St. Catharines Public Library, Linda Kurki and Arden Phair, from the St. Catharines Museum, and Andrew Porteus, from the Niagara Falls Public Library, for their assistance in tracking down relevant materials.

The financial support of Brock University, particularly the university's Jobs and Justice Research Unit, was greatly appreciated.

Finally, we thank labour activists in Niagara, past and present, who helped shape the content of this book with their stories of struggle and solidarity.

# Abbreviations

| | |
|---|---|
| **AFL** | American Federation of Labor |
| **AWA** | Agricultural Workers Alliance |
| **CAW** | Canadian Auto Workers |
| **CCF** | Co-operative Commonwealth Federation |
| **CCL** | Canadian Congress of Labour |
| **CEP** | Communications, Energy and Paperworkers |
| **CIO** | Congress of Industrial Organizations |
| **CLC** | Canadian Labour Congress |
| **CNH** | Canadian Niagara Hotels |
| **CPU** | Canadian Paperworkers Union |
| **CUPE** | Canadian Union of Public Employees |
| **GHSAC** | Golden Horseshoe Social Action Committee |
| **GM** | General Motors |
| **GROW** | Growing Respect for Offshore Workers |
| **HERE** | Hotel, Motel and Restaurant Employees Union |
| **IAM** | International Association of Machinists and Aerospace Workers |
| **IATSE** | International Alliance of Theatrical Stage Employees |
| **ILGWU** | International Ladies' Garment Workers' Union |
| **ILP** | Independent Labor Party |

| | |
|---|---|
| **IWA** | International Woodworkers of America |
| **LIUNA** | Laborers' International Union of North America |
| **MP** | Member of Parliament |
| **MPP** | Member of Provincial Parliament |
| **NDP** | New Democratic Party |
| **OFL** | Ontario Federation of Labour |
| **OLRB** | Ontario Labour Relations Board |
| **OPSEU** | Ontario Public Service Employees Union |
| **OSSTF** | Ontario Secondary School Teachers Federation |
| **PCC** | Plymouth Cordage Company |
| **RWDSU** | Retail, Wholesale and Department Store Union |
| **SAWP** | Seasonal Agricultural Workers Program |
| **TLC** | Trades and Labor Congress |
| **UAW** | United Automobile Workers of America |
| **UE** | United Electrical, Radio and Machine Workers Union |
| **UFCW** | United Food and Commercial Workers Union |
| **UNITE** | Union of Needletrades, Industrial and Textile Employees |
| **USWA** | United Steelworkers of America |
| **UTWA** | United Textile Workers of America |

# UNION
# POWER

# Introduction

"Who's got the power? We've got the power! What kind of power? Union power!" This call-and-response chant could be heard loud and clear at a 16 June 2007 rally in support of hotel workers in the heart of the Niagara Falls tourism district. UNITE HERE Local 2347, the union representing room attendants, servers, cooks, and bellhops working for three area hotels owned by Canadian Niagara Hotels, was locked in an intense and prolonged dispute with hotel management over intimidation of union activists, the unfair imposition of split shifts, and the non-payment of salary increases and negotiated bonuses.

Autoworkers, steelworkers, teachers, public service workers, postal workers, and university workers from across Niagara and throughout the province converged on the Sheraton on the Falls hotel in solidarity with the hotel workers to send a message to the hotel owners that the union was not going to back down without a fight. Union members and their allies peacefully marched through the streets waving flags and carrying banners demanding respect and dignity for hotel and hospitality workers. Different unions at the rally pledged their unwavering support for Local 2347 in its struggle against hotel management, emphasizing the need to stick together, stay strong, and keep up the fight.

Individually, workers have little bargaining power at work and little political power in their communities. When workers join together in unions, however, their collective voices have greater potential to shape and influence both the terms and conditions of their employment and the broader political, social, and economic spheres in which their employment relationships are embedded. Unlike corporate power, union power is not built on profit, status, or prestige. Instead, at its core, union power relies on the twin concepts of struggle and solidarity. Union and working-class solidarity is premised on the idea that workers have shared class interests and must struggle together, as a class, to achieve their goals. Where solidarity is strong, and the struggle is intense, union power is enhanced.

Niagara's rich labour history is full of examples of union power. In some cases, as in Local 2347's fight to defend its existence, workers managed to combat corporate power effectively. In other cases, especially when employers have been able to exploit divisions internal to the working class, whether based on ideology, race, or gender, union power has been weakened considerably, and the labour movement has lost ground. This book recounts and reflects on some of the pivotal union struggles and displays of working-class solidarity, past and present, that have shaped the character of Niagara's labour movement. Although, on occasion, workers from across the peninsula have acted collectively on their own behalf, more often union struggles have taken place in individual workplaces and communities.

## Niagara Region Municipal Boundaries

The Niagara region, 2011. Courtesy of the Brock University Map Library.

Niagara Peninsula Conservation Authority map
of the Niagara area, 1955. Courtesy of the
Niagara Peninsula Conservation Authority.

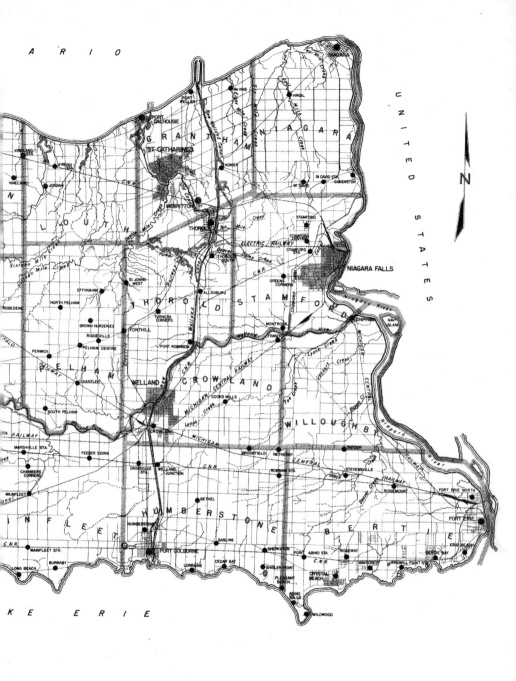

# Canallers Fight for Work and Fair Wages

The right to work and fair wages have been workers' goals since the earliest development of commercial capitalism in Niagara. Large numbers of waged workers first came to this area during the construction of the Welland Canal, which began in 1827. A few of these workers were skilled, such as the stonemasons who built dams and masonry locks, but the majority were unskilled labourers. Their work was both physically demanding and dangerous, much of it still completed by hand with the aid of such traditional tools as picks, shovels, axes, and wheelbarrows and animals for hauling. Accidents, especially those resulting from the use of explosives, could lead to injuries and even death. Canallers worked fourteen to sixteen hours a day, six days a week, in extreme heat in the summer and bitter cold in the winter. But the work was not steady, and if bad weather prevented them from working, they were not paid at all. Furthermore, the availability of work shrank during the winter months, and the resulting surplus of workers allowed contractors to force down wages. Some contractors paid their workers not in cash but in vouchers, redeemable only in overpriced provisions from stores run by the contractors themselves. Having underestimated the cost of building their section of the canal during the course of intense bidding with competitors, some contractors ran out of money and fled without paying the workers. But even those canallers who were able to work fairly regularly lived near subsistence level, most often in shacks along the waterway. When this phase of building ended, many of them migrated to other public building projects in search of work.[1]

By the time work on the second canal began in 1842, a reduction of canal construction in the northeastern United States created a huge surplus of canallers, many of whom came to Niagara in search of work. Their number was increased by new immigrants, primarily from Ireland. As a result, thousands of these workers could not find work, and they were so destitute that they were unable to leave Niagara to look elsewhere for work. In the absence of a public relief system in Upper Canada, they turned to begging and, in desperation, even to stealing from more established area residents. Soon the area's permanent residents began to suffer from what we would describe today as compassion fatigue. Although locals understood that the labourers' extreme poverty motivated their begging and petty theft, they increasingly viewed them with suspicion.[2]

Common labourers were vulnerable to exploitation because, lacking specialized skills, they were easy to replace. Sometimes the labourers reacted to the shortage of work by fighting for scarce jobs among themselves; at other times, however, they united to demand work and fair wages. In the summer of 1842, for example, they withheld their labour, demanding work for all. They put up posters along the canal reading, "Death and vengeance to any who should dare to work until employment is given to the whole." To reinforce these threats, bands of workers patrolled the canal and drove off anyone who tried to work.[3] Several thousand labourers took their complaints to nearby St. Catharines, parading through the streets bearing a red flag and a sign demanding "Bread or Work." On this occasion, the superintendent of the Welland Canal responded by providing additional work by expanding construction. A year later, in July 1843, canal workers went on strike again, demanding — and winning — higher wages. But, given the fluctuations in canal work, such successes could not last. By November of that year, wages had been rolled back, and the competition for scarce jobs led to such violent fights among canallers from different parts of Ireland that the militia was called in. The *St. Catharines Journal* described the belligerents as "strange" and "mad factions . . . thirsting like savages for each other's blood."[4] Canallers, who threatened to attack passengers on boats passing through the canal, also interfered with navigation. The government of the United Province of Canada and the board that oversaw canal construction perceived the canallers' actions as such a serious threat to the local economy that they joined forces with the contractors to suppress labour protests. They compiled blacklists to prevent the hiring of labour activists. The government passed legislation forbidding canallers to carry arms, and the board hired mounted police to keep labourers in line.[5] During the early stages of capitalist development, in short, unskilled workers occasionally acted together along class lines, but their collective strength was insufficient to counter employers backed by the state. They were not yet able to secure significant improvements in their condition.

# The Early Labour Movement

In the second half of the nineteenth century, the Niagara Peninsula became a hub of manufacturing. Water power, increased settlement, rich agricultural surroundings, closeness to American markets, and the construction of railway lines all contributed to the area's economic development. Following Confederation, when John A. Macdonald's government imposed tariffs on American-made goods to protect the development of Canadian manufacturing from competition, branches of American plants were also established in the area. Canneries, flour mills, breweries, and tanneries processed the district's agricultural products. Farm implements factories, foundries, machine shops, and basket makers provided local farmers with tools and containers. Sawmills and paper mills relied on wood transported to the area by rail and water. Textile and rubber factories, carriage and bicycle makers, shipbuilders, and cigar makers constituted other early manufacturing establishments in the Niagara region. Niagara Falls, St. Catharines, Thorold, and Welland developed as the larger manufacturing and service centres of the peninsula.

Company picnic for Queenston Quarry workers, 1890.
Courtesy of the Niagara Falls (Ontario) Public Library (D417717).

In contrast to the unskilled, itinerant canal workers of earlier decades, skilled workers such as cigar makers, coopers, machinists, iron moulders, printers, and shoemakers enjoyed a fair degree of autonomy in their working lives. By the 1870s, skilled workers in St. Catharines had established branches of the Amalgamated Society of Engineers, the Amalgamated Society of Carpenters and Joiners, and the International Typographical Union. The town was also the Canadian headquarters of the union of shoe factory workers, the Knights of St. Crispin. In Welland, printers and stonecutters established unions during the same period. Their skill and organization allowed such workers, virtually all of whom were male, to exercise some control over their hours of work, their wages, and the number of apprentices taken on in their trades. The case of cigar makers in St. Catharines illustrates the benefits of unionization. In the 1880s, when non-unionized workers toiled as long as fourteen hours a day, cigar makers in St. Catharines worked an eight-hour day. While some unorganized workers were still paid irregularly and in vouchers, these cigar makers received cash wages every week. Perhaps nothing illustrates the power of organized cigar makers better than their ability to prevent the local sale of cigars made cheaply by girls and boys in London (Ontario) and Montréal. Despite their higher cost, only union-made cigars could be found in the city. Given that cigar manufacturers often started out as journeymen cigar makers, having completed an apprenticeship in the trade, and cigar factories were still rather small, relations between employers and workers in this industry appeared cordial. In 1887, a St. Catharines cigar manufacturer pronounced union men more reliable, sober, and industrious than their non-unionized counterparts.[1]

Even during the period of early industrialization, however, there were limits to the harmony between workers and employers. When St. Catharines employers, facing greater competition in an increasingly integrated market, attempted to lower the costs of production by lowering wages or breaking down the process of production, the threat of a strike was frequently enough to persuade them to change their minds. Skilled workers, moreover, did not hesitate to lay down their tools during conflicts with employers who defied threats. Some employers responded by bringing in workers from Toronto's immigration sheds to replace militant workers, or by threatening to do so.

The ranks of unskilled workers, among them many women and children, in textile, garment, and canning factories and in the wood and iron industries, enjoyed none of the advantages of skilled, unionized workers like the St. Catharines cigar makers. Their wages were low, their working hours long, and their working conditions at times appalling. Canneries in Grimsby employed children as young as eight. Fifteen- and sixteen-year-old boys, whose income was needed by their families and who found jobs in the wood and iron industries, were forced to operate machines with inadequate training, they suffered frequent injuries, sometimes losing fingers and even hands. To make ends meet, women and girls in the garment industry often had to take work home and sew late into the night.[2]

Adult women's wages were so low partly because their work was seen as unskilled. Unlike tradesmen's skills, acquired through years of apprenticeship, women's work in the clothing and food-processing industries, and as domestics, cooks, kitchen help, waitresses, and chamber maids in Niagara homes and hotels, supposedly required no training. Such work was seen as a mere extension of work they performed in the home. Whatever skills such work required, such as attentiveness to detail or nimble fingers, were believed to come naturally to women. Both employers and male workers, moreover, considered women secondary wage earners. Working men aspired to earn enough so that their wives and children would not have to go out to work. They wanted to protect women and children from the harsh working conditions in factories. Indeed, the ideal of working-class masculinity rested on the notion that the male head would act as provider and protector of his family. But male workers also wanted to ensure that employers could not use women and children as low-wage competitors for "men's jobs." Whatever the goals of male workers, their idea of a family wage reinforced women's financial dependence on men. Employers could justify paying women low wages on the grounds that they were merely supplementing the income of their family's principal male bread-winner. Not surprisingly, most working-class women, once they married, withdrew from formal paid employment. Performing unpaid domestic work made more practical sense than staying in poorly paid jobs. Through careful shopping, keeping a garden and sometimes domestic animals, and preserving foods, women could stretch the wages that their husbands and children earned. Some women also sewed garments, made boxes, kept boarders, and/or took in laundry to add to their family income.[3]

With the arrival of the Noble and Holy Order of the Knights of Labor in Niagara in the 1880s, unskilled workers, including women, could join the labour movement. First established in the United States, the organization enjoyed rapid growth in Ontario, and in Niagara specifically, because of the rapid expansion of manufactur-ing at the time and the relative homogeneity of Niagara's working class. In the 1880s, most Niagara workers were English-speaking, and their ranks included British immigrants with considerable prior experience in labour organizations. Some of the Knights' assemblies (similar to union locals) were still made up of work-ers belonging to a single craft, some brought together skilled and unskilled workers in a given industry, and some, the so-called "mixed" assemblies, were composed of different types of workers. In principle, the Knights of Labor was open to all workers, regardless of skill, gender, or race. In practice, its policies toward women and racialized minorities were contradictory. The Knights were genuinely committed to improving the fate of women workers, arguing that women deserved the same pay as men. The organization also supported equal political rights for women, roughly three decades before Canadian women actually obtained the right to vote. Male Knights, however, also saw themselves as the protectors of the "weaker" female sex and continued to believe that women's proper place was in the home.[4] As for racialized groups, although we have no evidence of African Canadians belonging to assemblies in the Niagara region, we know that a number of assemblies in Toronto had black members. Yet in both Canada and the United States, the Knights were also not immune to a wider racism that called for the exclusion of people of Asian origin from North America.[5]

The organization's agenda — to improve the condition of workers by limiting the hours of work, advocating temperance, promoting education through a labour press and other publications, replacing competitive individualism with the spirit of cooperation, and giving workers a voice in politics — clearly appealed to workers in Niagara. Over two thousand workers established twenty-three locals of the Knights of Labor in the Niagara Peninsula. St. Catharines had eight assemblies, representing coopers, tailors, sailors, clerks, axe makers, and wheel makers, as well as a mixed assembly, comprising various trades. Thorold, which at that time had only three hundred industrial workers, had three assemblies: one of stonecutters employed in the local quarry, one mixed, and one made up of women. Merritton's Maple Leaf Assembly was the largest in the area, comprising five hundred cotton workers, many of them women. Sailors from Port Dalhousie and the Welland Canal, stonecutters from Beamsville and Welland, and railroad employees from the villages of Clifton, International Bridge, and York also joined the Knights of Labor.[6]

Knights from the Niagara Peninsula expressed their commitment to the organization's goals by electing one of their own, William Garson — a member of St. Catharines Fidelity Assembly, temperance advocate, and well-known Orangeman — as a Liberal-Labour member of the provincial legislature in 1886.[7] Garson expressed the Knights' desire to unite all workers by urging Protestant and Catholic workers to overcome sectarian divisions. On 15 August 1887, the Knights marked a civic holiday by marching 3,000 strong through the streets of St. Catharines, carrying banners that proclaimed "Rise and Defend Your Dignity," "The Land for the People," and "Long Hours Must Go."[8] In 1888, they fought to end long hours for store clerks by pledging to patronize only stores that closed at six o'clock in the evening.[9] In the same year, respect for the Christian Sabbath, as well as concern for workers operating the Welland Canal, led them to condemn the canal's operation on Sunday. In addition to working and fighting together for a better world, Niagara Knights also played together. Balls, dances, and roller-skating parties served not only to offer alcohol-free entertainment but also to raise funds to help disabled workers.[10]

Like their attitudes toward women workers and racialized minorities, the Knights' view of strikes was also contradictory. In principle, they favoured arbitration as a way of settling conflict between employers and workers. But when faced with stubborn employers, members of the organization did resort to strikes. For example, when John S. McClelland, a printer and a member of the Knights, purchased the *Evening Star*, a St. Catharines paper, in 1888 and refused to pay union wages, all but three of his printers went on strike. However, neither McClelland — who berated the strikers in the columns of his paper — nor the three strike-breaking printers were kicked out of the Knights of Labor. This lack of action led other workers to leave the Knights in disappointment.[11] By then, however, the organization's influence was decreasing in Niagara, as well as in many other parts of Canada and the United States. An economic downturn and disagreements within the organization were two of the main reasons for its decline.

# Class and Ethnicity in the
# Early Twentieth Century

Proximity to cheap electricity, generated by the large hydro stations at Niagara Falls and Decew Falls, drew industrial employers to the Niagara Peninsula during the last decades of the nineteenth and the first decade of the twentieth centuries. The imposition of tariffs on manufactured goods from the United States in the late nineteenth century, combined with proximity to the border, provided added incentive for American companies to establish branch plants in the Niagara Peninsula. Incentives from different communities in the form of bonuses, tax exemptions or fixed taxation, inexpensive hydro rates, and free links to sewage and water played a key role in determining where in the region employers built their factories. Both the number and size of local industries grew as new technology allowed employers to replace skilled workers with machines tended by semi-skilled workers. Although each of the larger communities in the peninsula attracted a variety of industries, a certain degree of specialization became evident among them. St Catharines became the centre of automobile parts manufacturing, chemical and allied industries located in Niagara Falls and Chippawa, metal and metal fabricating industries were Welland's largest employers, Thorold and Merriton attracted large paper mills, while Port Colborne became a centre of flour milling and metal smelting. Construction of the hydro canals and power-generating stations, the new factories, and the fourth Welland Canal created additional demand for labour.[1]

Because the industrial boom coincided with a dramatic increase in immigration from southern and eastern Europe, many of the new industrial and construction jobs were filled by immigrant workers. Armenians, Hungarians, Italians, Poles, and Ukrainians were some of the larger groups to migrate to Niagara at this time. The region appealed to these immigrants because, in the event of a downturn in industry, the large construction projects connected with power development and the Welland Canal, as well as seasonal work in agriculture and canning, provided alternative local employment opportunities. Immigrants could thus save the time and expense of moving elsewhere in search of work. They took the least skilled, least secure, lowest paid, and most physically demanding jobs in manufacturing and large public works projects, partly because many were former agriculturalists without previous experience in factory work. Most were also sojourners, temporary residents who intended to work in Canada only long enough to save enough money to permit them to improve their situation when they returned to their native lands. Because they did not plan to stay at these jobs for long, they often put up with conditions that more established Canadian workers would have found intolerable.

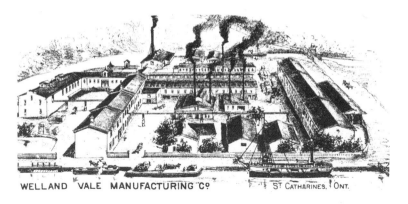

WELLAND VALE MANUFACTURING C?     ST CATHARINES. ONT.

Welland Vale Manufacturing Company, makers of agricultural
implements, tools, and bicycles, established in 1901.
Courtesy of the St. Catharines Public Library, Special Collections.

Even if they decided to settle in Canada, however, these immigrants had little chance of getting better jobs. Starting in the early twentieth century, the racializing of immigrant workers — attributing to them substantial, inborn characteristics that distinguished them from others — became even more significant in the development of Niagara's labour movement than it had been during the building of the second Welland Canal in the 1840s. Many of their employers, fellow workers, and other Canadians believed that southern and eastern Europeans, and especially those of Asian and African origin, were racially inferior and equipped to perform only menial labour.

McKinnon Industries, for example, recruited Armenian workers from the United States specifically to carry out hot and heavy work in its foundry, which became known as "Little Armenia." [2] Poles, Italians, Ukrainians, Hungarians, and other immigrants from southern and eastern Europe joined the Armenians in the foundry and in other unskilled jobs. During World War II, when labour shortages enabled European immigrant workers to move to better-paying and less arduous jobs, the company recruited blacks from Nova Scotia for its foundry.

Employers in Niagara, as elsewhere in Canada during this period, attempted to use racism to their own ends. The first large American manufacturer to locate in Welland — the Plymouth Cordage Company, makers of rope and binder twine — encouraged northern Italian employees from Plymouth, Massachusetts, to relocate to Welland and to invite relatives from Italy to join them there. This move was financially important for the employers because these supposedly unskilled immigrant workers possessed skills in ropemaking that the company would have otherwise had to pay new hires to acquire.[3] The company also believed that hiring based on family and ethnic ties would strengthen worker loyalty.[4] At the same time, however, the company's officers took ethnic inequality so much for granted that they did not consider placing their experienced Italian workers in responsible positions such as that of foreman within their Welland plant. Instead, they proposed to send forty or fifty local Anglo-Canadians with no experience in ropemaking to Plymouth, Massachusetts, to train for these positions. They advertised their plans in the *Welland Telegraph*, probably to appeal to the sense of superiority and entitlement to local jobs felt by Welland's Anglo-Canadian workers.[5] They gave little thought to how their Italian employees might view this policy.

Such evident discrimination undermined or at least challenged the loyalty of workers of Italian origin. Some of the workers who agreed to relocate to Welland did so because they hoped to improve their jobs. They were sorely disappointed. Flavio Botari, the son of one of the leaders of the original group of Italian workers from Plymouth, remembered that his older brother, who was "clever mechanically," found that he was "hitting his head against the ceiling because he was quite low on the promotion scale" at the company. "The sons of the white Anglo-Saxons were always ahead of him, and he never got a chance to get into the machine shop that he wanted to go into. He always felt that people with a lot less talent were being promoted ahead of him, so he left."[6] Botari's reference to "white" Anglo-Saxons, to distinguish them from Italian workers, illustrates the nature of racialization in this period. Esch Orsini, of the same generation as Flavio Botari, recalled his parents' observation that one became a foreman at Plymouth Cordage only "if you were 'one of them,' one of the Anglo-Saxons."[7]

Plans for worker housing also reflected the employer's assumptions of racial hierarchy. Welland, still a very small town in 1905, could not accommodate the influx of workers. Consequently, the Plymouth Cordage Company built new housing for its workers. Over one hundred families were housed in three large single-family homes, twenty-four duplexes, ten four-unit buildings, and a large boarding house. Flavio Botari described how the hierarchy at Plymouth Cordage manifested itself in the configuration of company housing. The residents of the "upper crust section" were Anglo-Saxons: the foremen, office workers, and the painters and carpenters who performed maintenance work on the company housing. Almost all residents of the four tenement houses were Italian, with the rest consisting of a Portuguese, a Spaniard, and a Romanian, as well as one or two French Canadian families, all of whom came up from Plymouth. The single male workers housed in the boarding house were also mostly Italians.[8]

Plymouth Cordage boardinghouse for single male workers.
Courtesy of the Welland Public Library.

Plymouth Cordage Company dwelling houses on Muir Street (above),
and cottages on First Street (below), Welland, Ontario.
Courtesy of the Welland Public Library

The Plymouth Cordage Company was not alone in its race-based housing policies. Another Welland employer, the Canadian Steel Company, built a separate lodging house for its "foreign" workers and employed an Italian immigrant to run it.[9] In neighbouring

Thorold, the British-owned Pilkington Glass Company, a manufacturer of sheet and plate glass, brought most of its tradesmen from its plant in the United Kingdom and built housing for them in the planned community of Windle Village.[10] It made no such provisions for the ordinary labourers in its employ. The men, principally Italians, Romanians, and Bulgarians, built rough shacks from old lumber and tar paper for themselves. Without adequate services, they found it difficult to maintain sanitary living conditions in their dwellings.[11] The Norton Company, a manufacturer of abrasives in Chippawa, also built housing for its workers, constructing individual cottages for its Anglo-Canadian workers and lodging houses for "foreigners."[12] During this boom period, Niagara developers assumed that local residents of British origin, whatever their class, probably shared the employers' views. This is why the developer of a "better class of houses for working men" in Maple Leaf Park, Crowland, advertised the subdivision as "restricted," assuring prospective buyers that "you will have no foreign element building or living next to you."[13] Even if "foreigners" had been able to afford homes in better neighbourhoods, restrictive covenants excluded them, thus reinforcing segregation. Consequently, immigrant factory workers who were not accommodated by company housing rented and built homes in "foreign quarters," often on the outskirts of Niagara towns and villages, in the shadow of large factories. Soot from the factories covered their homes and gardens. Such neighbourhoods also lacked essential services such as sewers, sidewalks, and fire protection.

Employers' exploitation of ethnic differences became most clearly apparent during strikes, when they recruited strikebreakers. In 1899, a strike by trackmen near Port Robinson for higher wages and shorter hours spread to other rail workers in the area. The Grand Trunk Railway responded by bringing in three coaches fitted up as living accommodations and filled with workers, some of them Italian, to replace the strikers. In this case, the plan failed. As Welland's *People's Press* reported, "Three prominent ladies of the town went out to the cars and made the men so ashamed of themselves that they left." The paper added that "the sympathy of the whole village here is with the men who have struck for a living wage, and it is not thought any further attempt will be made to replace them here."[14] Four years later, "foreign" labourers, described as Italians and "Huns," were imported from Buffalo to replace striking workers in the Sherkston quarry, between Port Colborne and Ridgeway. According to the *Welland Telegraph*, the government refused to enforce the federal Alien Labour Act, which prohibited the importation of contract labour. An angry editorial in the paper demanded: "Is it right that respectable Canadian citizens, the heads of families, should be compelled to compete for work with gangs of aliens whose mode of living is hardly above the Chinese standard?"[15]

Ethnically based inequality was also pronounced among workers on the large public works projects in Niagara: provincial hydro canals and generating stations and the federally funded construction of the fourth Welland Canal, each of which employed thousands of workers in the early twentieth century. The skilled workers among them, such as carpenters, machinists, electricians, masons, and operating engineers, were of British descent; the majority of common labourers were non–Anglo-Celtic. The skilled workers belonged to such well-established craft unions as the United Brotherhood of Carpenters and Joiners, the United Association of Plumbers and Steamfitters, and the International Association of Machinists. These unions monitored wages and hours on public works projects and attempted to ensure that they were consistent with those elsewhere in the Niagara Peninsula. When the unions called a strike, they could encourage the participation of tradesmen by threatening them with fines and blacklisting throughout the region if they continued to work. During the years of labour protest between 1918 and 1920, the "foreign" workers, with some exceptions, were unorganized. Consequently, they could be more easily replaced by returning soldiers and native-born workers at the end of the war, when the demand for labour along the canals became less acute.[16]

Canadian Niagara Power Plant workers excavating through rock for the wheel pit, 1902. Courtesy of the Niagara Falls (Ontario) Public Library (D415450C).

The early-twentieth-century immigrant canal workers, not unlike the Irish canallers of the nineteenth century, remained on the margins of Niagara society. They lived in shacks, converted barns, bunkhouses, and sometimes even tents near construction sites or in crowded housing in the "foreign quarters" of local towns and villages such as Crowland, Humberstone, Niagara Falls, Stamford, St. Catharines, Thorold, and Welland. By contrast, many of the skilled canal workers were local men who lived with their own families or boarded with Anglo-Canadian ones in communities along the canals. Those who could not find such accommodations were housed in contractor-built camps that were separate from, and slightly more expensive and comfortable than, those for "foreigners." Because boarding workers was not particularly profitable, contractors preferred to pass on the task when they could. The gender imbalance among sojourners worked to the contractors' advantage. Given the racism prevalent in Niagara, and their own poverty, often the only way that the few immigrant women who accompanied canal workers could find housing was by agreeing to run boarding houses for southern and eastern European immigrants.[17]

In 1910, the tragic death by fire of twelve foreign-born workers in Falls View village, near Niagara Falls, drew public attention to living conditions in the "foreigners" camps. The men lived in overcrowded tarpaper shacks with earthen floors, a few small windows, and narrow doors that opened inward. One of the shacks had sleeping accommodations for eighteen, but it housed twice that number. The female boarding-house keeper explained that "only 18 sleep at one time as the day shift gets into the same beds the night shift vacates."[18] Such overcrowding of working men who lacked proper facilities for washing themselves and their clothes created an atmosphere replete not only with unpleasant odours but also with diseases, some of them contagious. A Roman Catholic priest who visited the shacks before the fire found a man dying of tuberculosis lying a foot away from other boarders, who did their best to tend to him.[19] A fireman called to the scene of the blaze commented that the shacks were "just made to burn up." The horrific tragedy temporarily breached the gulf that separated mainstream Niagara society from the "foreigners." The Niagara Falls *Daily Record* declared, "Deserted and isolated, neglected by the authorities and the denominations alike and constantly subjected to the fatal risks of fire and disease 150 men of foreign birth are living the lives of outcasts from civilization just beyond the corporate limits of this city." It blamed not only the Stamford officials who allowed all township sanitary and safety regulations to be ignored but also the Niagara Falls residents who owned the shacks. The paper expressed outrage at the decision of the local coroner not to conduct an inquest following the fire: "We join our voice with those of the twelve dead laborers and ask the coroner a single question. Why?"[20]

Race-based inequality was pronounced in Niagara's important agricultural sector as well. Local farmers employed Anglo-Celtic farm help who worked the year round, but most of the seasonal agricultural and cannery workers they hired were of southern and eastern European origin. Although in Niagara there were few openings for year-round farm help, immigration officials went to great lengths to recruit agricultural workers from Great Britain to fill them.[21] The recruitment of seasonal farm labour was generally left to the farmers. Because such jobs involved backbreaking work for long periods, at times up to sixteen hours a day, for wages that were lower than those for almost any other type of work in the region, farmers could not always find enough workers locally. Before the First World War, some farmers traveled to Buffalo in the harvest season to find immigrant women to work as fruit pickers and in canneries. According to the 1911 census, 80 percent of those employed in the canning industry were female, some of them girls as young as twelve. Accommodation for these workers, if provided, was generally primitive. Gender-based paternalism, moreover, placed serious limits on the freedom of female workers. Some of them were housed in compounds, in bunkhouses built right next to the canning factories, and were not allowed to leave the compounds after eight o'clock in the evening. A 1915 survey on the condition of female agricultural workers, prepared by the Department of Social Service and Evangelism of the Methodist and Presbyterian Church, likened the terms of their employment to slavery.[22]

# Labour Revolt in Niagara

Although immigrant sojourners were more likely to put up with working and living conditions that workers with greater options disdained, there were limits to what they were willing to endure. Since their goal was to earn as much money as quickly as possible so that they could return to their homelands with savings, they reacted especially strongly when employers attempted to reduce their wages. In 1903, for example, eight hundred workers employed by the power development works in Niagara Falls — mostly Hungarians, Italians, and Poles — responded to notices of wage cuts for common labour by striking. To prevent the resumption of work, they marched up and down the work sites along the Niagara River, their radical sympathies expressed by the red cloth attached to a pole that their leader carried. After the strike was quelled by the militia, hundreds of strikers continued their protest by leaving Niagara, mostly for the United States.[1]

Although such immigrants left few written records of their aspirations, we have some indications that their protests were not simply spontaneous reactions to the actions of their employers. A few of the immigrants had sufficient command of English to express their views to Anglo-Canadians. The language of Andreas Muellers, who described himself as a "shack lodger" in a letter to the *Daily Record* following the deadly Falls View fire, may have been grammatically imperfect, but his allegation of criminal negligence in the housing of immigrant workers was well informed and convincing:

> Do you know mister editor that they puts 25 mans in a shack and the windows don't open and the door opens in. When the mans go to get out, no door open, men all burn. I wants to say every shack here is breaking the rule and all the doors open in. They some so small only 1 mans can go out at once. Theys got a shack with 65 people here, windows so high no man can reach only one door it open in. Do you allow that kind of things to go on, do you allow that to go in your churches, in your theatres, your schools. My country got to have things right or no allow to build.[2]

In his testimony before the 1920 Ontario government commission to investigate labour conditions on the Ontario Hydro-Electric Power Commission's Chippawa-Queenston Canal, a Bulgarian labourer spoke for many immigrant workers. He explained that because he spoke several languages, other men came to him with their complaints. They compared their work and wages with those of railway construction workers and concluded that the wages paid by the publicly owned Hydro Commission were unfairly low. Canal workers believed that the work they performed as pick and shovel men was much harder than work on railway lines and should therefore garner higher wages. They also protested that their wages were not enough to live on. The Bulgarian witness pointed out that, although he himself wanted to stay in Canada and bring his wife and children from Bulgaria to join him, he could not afford do so on his current wages.[3] Crowland's "Austrians," who informed a census taker in 1911, only two years after they arrived in Canada, that their religion was "socialist," most likely developed their ideological views in their country of origin. The same may have been true of the Niagara Ukrainians who attracted the attention of the police in 1920 by subscribing to anarchist newspapers.[4]

Anglo-Canadian workers initially responded with hostility when large numbers of southern and eastern European immigrants arrived in Niagara. Fears that employers would use the immigrants to deskill labour and reduce wages intensified Anglo-Canadian working-class racism. A letter signed "Laborer," written to the *Welland Telegraph* in 1903, after Italian and Hungarian workers were brought from the United States to work in the local quarry, illustrates such concerns:

> Why is it that foreign workmen are allowed to come to Canada and dispossess Canadian laborers, and are even given the preference over them? . . . Why is it that alien recruits are brought here in troops from Buffalo and other American cities to work on Canadian soil — a people who are strangers to our language and our laws; who have no sympathy with our institutions; who desecrate our Sabbaths and are notorious for their bibulous propensities.

"Laborer's" attitudes toward immigrant workers formed an integral part of his class consciousness — one that excluded "foreigners." He believed that Canadian law protected the "wealthy railroad corporations, grasping monopolists and oppressors of the poor" but failed to protect the worker by enforcing the Alien Labour Act.[5] In 1908, the District Trades and Labour Council of St. Catharines demanded the punishment of two local canning companies for violating the act by bringing their workers from the United States.[6] Gradually, however, many Anglo-Canadian labour activists realized that, to be effective, they would have to cooperate with the "foreign" workers. In 1916, six hundred unorganized workers on the Welland Canal — Russians, Bulgarians, Italians, and Austrians — struck for higher wages, and the federal government sent in soldiers "with fixed bayonets" to put down the strike. The *Industrial Banner,* a labour paper based in London, Ontario, pointed out that while the government did not hesitate to use the militia to protect employers, it never did so to defend workers' rights. The paper added that the government could act this way against foreign labourers because, unlike Anglo-Canadian tradesmen, they were ignorant and consequently "without organization or vote."[7] Toward the end of the First World War, however, when labour shortages improved the bargaining position of both native and immigrant workers, they joined unions in increasing numbers. Formed in 1918, the Niagara District Trades Federation represented both Canadian and foreign-born skilled and unskilled workers in the region. The secretary of the Trades and Labour Congress (TLC) of Niagara Falls explained the inclusion of foreigners:

> It is quite true that most of the men engaged on the hydro canal are foreigners because they do the work Canadians and Englishmen will not do. We have got to have them in these big works. Some criticism has been heard as to us taking them into the union. But we couldn't do otherwise seeing they must be employed. Further, eighty per cent of them are Italians — there are very few Austrians etc., and I have found that a majority of them are married men and are very anxious to bring their wives to Canada, but they are not making enough money to do so. Our idea is to get them enough money to bring their wives to Canada, establish homes and good Canadians can be made of these men.[8]

Workers throughout Canada asserted themselves in politics as well as in the workplace at the end of World War I. In St. Catharines many of them supported the Independent Labor Party (ILP), which emerged thanks to the notion — earlier advanced by the Knights of Labor — that only men from the working class could and would truly represent workers' interests at various levels of government. In the provincial election of 1919, St. Catharines sent Frank Greenlaw, an ILP member and trades council president, to the provincial legislature, now dominated by farmers and workers. They came close to sending another worker, an unemployed machinist, to Ottawa as well. Niagara Falls workers elected ILP candidate Charles F. Swayze, an accountant with labour sympathies, to represent them in the provincial legislature.[9]

Women exercising their newly won right to vote played an important role in the election of labour candidates. With the aid of Rose Henderson, a Montréal socialist, working-class women in St. Catharines organized political meetings where women without prior experience in public speaking spoke eloquently in support of political representation. Dozens of baby carriages and go-carts parked at the door of such meetings revealed that, if they had no child care, women simply brought their young children along. They also participated in the campaign by canvassing door-to-door and arranging child care on election day so that women could cast their votes at the polls.[10]

Two Niagara strikes during the period of labour militancy and radicalism that followed the First World War, often referred to as the period of Canada's "Labour Revolt," illustrate both the complex dynamics within the multiethnic labour movement and the relationship between organized workers and their ILP representatives in the United Farmers of Ontario government. The first of these strikes, by hydro canal workers at Chippawa in 1920, involved skilled and unskilled, immigrant and native-born workers. They demanded an eight-hour day and increased wages for working overtime and on Sundays. Their command of English enabled the Anglo-Canadian workers to articulate the grounds for these demands. A submarine driller told the commissioners that he believed he could do his work better and "not be cranky" with his children if he worked an eight-hour day.[11] An electrical locomotive engineer maintained that there would be fewer accidents on the canal if the work day was reduced to eight hours.[12] A fitter, secretary of the United Association of Plumbers and Steamfitters Local, argued that the canal workers' ambitions to improve themselves were thwarted by working ten hours a day. The Business Agent of the General Labourers and Drill Men's Local told the commissioners that labourers were too exhausted at the end of a ten-hour day to attend union meetings.[13] Although they left us no record of their motives, immigrant workers also supported these demands.

This interethnic collaboration, however, was insufficient to attain the hydro workers' goals. One of the commissioners, ILP member Malcolm MacBride, was sympathetic to the workers' arguments. He believed that local businesses, which had benefitted greatly from the availability of cheap power for a number of years, should be willing to pay a little more for power so that workers on the hydro projects could be paid fair wages.[14] In its report, however, the commission stated that the wages paid by the Hydro Commission compared favourably with wages paid elsewhere in Niagara and that the workers' housing conditions were "fairly satisfactory." The report supported the principle of the eight-hour day but argued that, in the interest of rapid completion of the canal, workers should be prepared to work ten hours a day at a rate of time-and-a-half for overtime.[15] The farmers' representative on the investigative commission, W. H. Casselman, disagreed, declaring that the eight-hour day was a "vicious principle."[16] Despite the unprecedented labour representation within it, the provincial government accepted the commission's findings. Moreover, when the hydro workers decided to strike, Niagara's ILP Members of Provincial Parliament Greenlaw and Swayze, along with MacBride, rushed to Niagara Falls to urge workers to stay on the job.[17] Concluding that the labour MPPs did not represent their interests, the workers struck. They returned to work nineteen days later, however, having won only minor concessions.

The tenuousness of the alliance between Anglo-Canadian and "foreign" workers became apparent a year later during a strike by Thorold workers. In 1921, workers of the Beaver Board Fibre Company in Thorold walked out when the company attempted to cut wages and return to an open shop (one in which union membership was not mandatory).[18] The strike leaders attempted to unite all Beaver Board workers by recruiting interpreters to address immigrants in their own languages. Despite their effort to transcend ethnic differences, however, the workers were unable to counter the combined power of employers and the state.

Beaver Board Company plant, Thorold, as pictured in *St. Catharines: An Industrial Survey* (1933). Courtesy of the Brock University Library, Special Collections and Archives.

The company almost immediately hired, and armed, special constables from an American detective agency, claiming they were needed to guard company property. The company also sent an agent to hire strikebreakers in the United States, despite the illegality of this practice under the Alien Labour Act. One of the strikebreakers testified that the company's man assured prospective recruits that "there would be no trouble getting across the International Bridge. He instructed me to say 'I am for the Beaver Board,' and it would be all right. 'We give them a box of cigars every Christmas.'" The company's agent added that the Canadian government supported the company in this strike. Indeed, when the company asked for six North-West Mounted Police, the government sent seventy-two policemen.[19]

Both the employers and state authorities, who had been happy enough to recruit "foreign" immigrants to perform unskilled, ill-paid jobs in factories and large public works in the area, did not hesitate to exploit racial and ethnic tensions to create divisions among the Beaver Board strikers. Ontario Provincial Police raided "foreign" workers' shacks and boarding houses, claiming that "nearly all the foreigners have fire-arms, and when they get drunk, they fire them off indiscriminately." They explained that the Thorold police were so afraid of the "foreigners" that they had become a "joke." When they went to arrest a "Russian" in his home, the occupants threw the local officers out of the window. Subsequently, the local police refrained from taking any action against "foreigners." Given these serious accusations against "dangerous" immigrant workers, it is noteworthy that the authorities could lodge no more serious charges against the seven picketers, a number of whom were of foreign descent, than vagrancy and calling the strikebreakers "scabs" and "rats." In response to the strong show of force by the company and the police, and their anti-foreign propaganda, the strike leaders distanced themselves from labour radicalism and blamed "foreigners" for the "danger of Bolshevism" in Thorold.[20]

Even when workers decided to try to overcome race-based divisions, the inclusiveness of the labour movement remained incomplete, as illustrated by the response of Welland workers to the Plymouth Cordage Company's decision in 1917 to employ two hundred Chinese workers. The company brought the workers to Welland from various parts of Canada after losing many of its workers to better paid jobs in other Niagara factories. According to a Welland alderman, the wages paid by the Plymouth Cordage Company at this time were "almost scandalous."[21] Workers of Chinese origin were willing to work for the company, because even low-waged manufacturing jobs — denied to them before the war by racist discrimination — still paid better than the jobs in small Chinese restaurants and laundries that they customarily filled. As Welland's *People's Press* explained, "They could make more a week, working for the Plymouth Cordage than in washing shirts."[22]

A large delegation of workingmen besieged the municipal council with other Welland residents to protest against the employment of Chinese workers in the city. One worker saw the importation of Chinese labourers as a continuation of the company's prewar practices: "Before the war the Cordage Company employed foreign labour in preference to British labour. The reason why manufacturers were employing Chinese today is because they are cheap." [23] The representative of the United Brotherhood of Carpenters and Joiners Local argued that "it would be shameful for the boys of Welland to come back" from the front only to "find the yellow races occupying the place that was legitimately theirs." Other citizens, whose class background was not identified by the local press, worried that the arrival of the Chinese would lead to a decline of local real estate values, create a negative impression of the city, and endanger the community's health and the safety of Welland's women. They proposed that the Chinese labourers be housed behind a fence on the company's property and be allowed onto the streets of Welland only two at a time.

Welland employers responded that labour shortages, combined with their strong sense of patriotism, were responsible for their reliance on workers of Chinese origin. The treasurer of the Plymouth Cordage Company explained that there was a serious shortage of twine to bind the country's grain crop. Pointing to the difficulty of finding labour, he offered pragmatic reasons for the company's hiring policies: "We believe a great responsibility rests on us and our patriotic duty is to employ every one available regardless of race, creed or color. Anything less would be slacking." John White of the Union Carbide Company advocated the employment of Chinese so that "white men" could be released for other work. F. C. Hesch of the Canada Forge attempted to relieve community anxiety by stating: "Just as soon as we can get sufficient labor to replace the Chinaman we will replace him. We do not use Chinamen to cheapen labor but because nothing else can be got." [24] Despite the protests, local manufacturers continued to employ Chinese labourers. At the war's end, most of these labourers left the area.

Labour's political strength in Niagara was short-lived. Labour MPPs found themselves powerless in Ontario's farmer-labour coalition government. When farmers and workers had been able to cooperate before and during the election, the differences in their goals had been muted, but tensions became apparent when their representatives assumed power. Farmers, for example, advocated free trade, whereas organized labour sought to maintain protective tariffs. As the junior partners in the farmer-labour coalition, workers had little say.

## Welfare Capitalism in Niagara

Alarmed by labour radicalism, employers meanwhile joined forces to defeat unionization. In Niagara, as elsewhere in industrial Ontario, they introduced corporate welfare schemes in an attempt to reduce class conflict. The most elaborate welfare plan in Niagara, that of the Plymouth Cordage Company, predated the First World War. As we have seen, the company provided housing for its workers in large measure because of the lack of worker housing in Welland in 1905. But such pragmatic considerations cannot explain the careful upkeep of the company housing: company employees painted and repaired the houses and the fencing around their gardens regularly. In winter they cleared the snow from roads and sidewalks and sold heating coal to company employees below market rates. Company recreational programs included a community hall, which housed a library, billiard tables, and a bowling alley for the workers, sewing and cooking classes for their daughters, and carpentry classes for their sons. The Plymouth Cordage band, comprised entirely of Italian workers, practiced at the hall. Workers and their families, many of them organized in company sports teams, had use of the tennis courts, football field, lawn bowling green, and supervised playground on the company grounds. At an annual fair, prizes were awarded to the company's workers for the best shade trees, vines, kitchen and flower gardens, poultry yards, drawing, photography, basketry, cooking, and for sporting achievements. The Plymouth Cordage Company also reached beyond its own employees. It demonstrated its commitment to the wider Welland community by donating land for a school site, to the local parks commission, and to the Methodist and Greek Orthodox churches, as well as by contributing funds for a local hospital.

Sloyd School, Plymouth Cordage Company plant, Welland, Ontario, ca. 1915. Courtesy of the Welland Historical Museum.

The welfare plan, imported from the United States, was decidedly paternalistic. As a company welfare official explained, encouraging workers to keep gardens, for example, was a way of encouraging good working habits: "Contact with the soil is healthy, it makes men constructive, because they see how much work it takes to produce, and how easy it is to destroy by neglect or badly directed effort."[1] The irony of purporting to rely on agricultural work to instil good working habits among workers of rural origin, who were all too familiar with such labour, completely escaped this official. He, like other managers of corporate welfare at this time, believed that "foreign" workers were especially in need of guidance. They attributed unrest among such workers to their "simple and childlike" nature, which explained why they were "easily led and stirred for good or for evil." [2] Their plans perpetuated existing class, race, and gender inequality. The Plymouth Cordage offered cooking classes for the daughters of its workers "to teach young girls how to prepare good food economically." [3] The company encouraged the participation of foremen, overseers, and workers in its men's club to promote harmonious relations and to help "make real men of all of us." [4]

While company housing and industrial nurses offered clear benefits to employees and their families, such policies also enhanced the company's ability to control and discipline workers. The threat of eviction could be invoked when management disapproved of a worker's conduct. A worker of Italian origin whose father worked at Plymouth Cordage recalled, for example, that the plant manager called him when his father's drinking started to interfere with his work. "Look," the manager told him, "you live in a company house, if he keeps this up we're gonna fire him." When his father continued drinking and the manager openly threatened to evict the family, the son saw no choice but to enter the company's employ himself. [5] The company's industrial nurse visited employees who stayed away from work partly to look after their health but also to ensure that they were not feigning illness.

A 1916 strike by Plymouth Cordage workers in Massachusetts brought changes to the company's welfare policies. It established an industrial relations department and introduced profit sharing in 1918. In 1931, it added a credit union, a sick benefit society, and an insurance plan, and, in 1934–35, a plant council, which brought together workers and management to discuss matters of concern to both parties. Company officials insisted that the new plan of industrial relations was fundamentally different from a paternalistic or welfare plan. They called it "social business." [6]

Yet despite all statements to the contrary, a paternalistic view of workers persisted after the new plan was introduced. C. P. Marshall, the company's industrial relations manager, called for the establishment of a company union — a union sponsored or at least endorsed by the company itself — as the only way to prevent the spread of independent trade unionism or socialism. In Marshall's words, the worker was "like a boy in the adolescent period" who wanted leadership to be told "why things are so." [7] The establishment of shop councils was necessary to take leadership away from the "professional leader" and the socialist and to make the shop, or factory, rather than class, the focus of the worker's loyalty. The same was true of the elaborate welfare scheme. As a company memo explained:

> Company housing, group life insurance, sickness insurance, wage retirement etc. are indirect wages. It would be simpler by far for the company to dispense the cost of these aids in cash but in that case the prospect of real betterment of employees would be lessened. Generally speaking if left to the working man reserves for his security would never be accumulated. [8]

According to F. C. Holmes, treasurer of the Plymouth Cordage Company, the plant council, established in Welland in 1935, merely gave formal expression to the spirit of cooperation and fair play that had always characterized relations between workers and management. The long-term interests of the employees and the company were, according to management, "the same, and not antagonistic." [9] The workers elected five representatives, who met with management to discuss matters of concern to them. The council's function was "to consider and make recommendations relating to policies." All policies, however, were put into effect by management, subject to review by the plant council. It was also made clear that this would sometimes mean cooperation with management "in the introduction of new methods of work." [10] In other words, the council would not simply act in an advisory capacity to management but would also help implement new policies, even if they were "for a time" unpopular. But there was another important reason that company unions offered workers far less power than did independent unions: they were restricted to single plants and therefore had access neither to information nor to financial aid from the wider labour movement. The absence of outside union support buttressed the power imbalance between employer and worker.

The records of the Plymouth Cordage council suggest that workers certainly did not feel free to express their concerns openly. For example, the council was supposed to guarantee representation without regard to race, sex, religion, or nationality. Yet one issue that the workers' representatives did not raise was the inability of non–Anglo-Celtic workers to obtain skilled positions and foremen's jobs. Indeed, the principle of seniority, which would have benefitted such workers, was not recognized by management. Instead, promotions, transfers, and layoffs were governed by "employee merit," on the basis of such criteria as "conduct, mental attitudes . . . adaptability, attendance, continuous service, citizenship and marital status, and personality," which left much up to the discretion of management.[11] While the council participated in decisions affecting working conditions, wages, hours of work, and employee benefits, implementation remained the prerogative of management, and decisions affecting wages were subject to revision when conditions changed. In practice, when workers requested wage increases or paid vacations, management sometimes responded that it could not afford to grant such requests and sometimes acceded to them. In the case of grievances concerning speed-ups, management justified its decisions by referring to "time studies."[12] This was probably an example of the kind of "temporarily unpopular" decisions to which Mr. Holmes referred.

At first glance, the company's welfare plan appeared to have succeeded. For half a century, Plymouth Cordage workers did not join a union, nor did they resort to strikes. Even years after the company ceased operations in Welland, moreover, its former employees and their children described the company as a good employer and fondly recalled its recreational programs. Some of them deemed the security of employment at the factory sufficient to make up for wages lower than those paid by other local manufacturers. "The company was known all over," recalled a former employee of Italian descent. "If you told anyone that you worked at the Cordage, you could get any amount of credit you wanted. They were a plant that, once you got a job there, you could almost say that you had a job for life."[13]

But workers' views of Plymouth Cordage welfare policies were not unequivocal. Housing undoubtedly provided an important incentive for staying at the Plymouth Cordage Company for some workers, even when better-paid jobs were available elsewhere. The quality of the housing should be considered in comparison to the shacks that housed so many other local workers at the time. As Welland's manufacturing sector grew, however, offering greater employment opportunities, often with higher wages than those at Plymouth Cordage, some workers, especially the children of the original group of employees, wanted to leave the company. The hope that their ethnicity would present less of an obstacle elsewhere, as well as the lower wages the company paid, drove immigrant workers to find other employment opportunities. In order to remain in company housing, however, at least one member of the household had to continue in Plymouth Cordage's employment. That is why one of the company's young workers, Esch Orsini, who first described the company's houses as "plums" and the company as having had tremendous vision in offering them to its workers, also referred to the Cordage houses as a "golden handcuff."[14]

The company's pension plan was another reason that some of the older workers stayed at Plymouth Cordage. They were sorely disappointed to discover, however, that the company's control over welfare plans meant that these benefits could be modified, suspended, or terminated at any time. Flavio Botari remembered that his father often mentioned "that there was a pension being put away for him by the company and that eventually, when he stopped work, that he would be collecting a pension," adding that "this was unusual too for those days." Despite long years of service to the Plymouth Cordage Company, both in Massachusetts and in Welland, the elder Botari did not receive a pension. To be eligible, he needed to have worked for the company for fifty years. The company let him go after forty-eight.[15]

Prosperity returned by the later 1920s, and a number of new industries, such as Hayes-Dana, Foster Wheeler, Thompson Products, Empire Rug Mills, and Grout's Silk Mills, emerged in the St. Catharines area. These were joined by Atlas Speciality Steel and Joseph Stokes Rubber Company in Welland, Fleet Industries in Fort Erie, and, in Niagara Falls, Brights Canning Company, Burgess Battery Company, and the Canadian Ohio Brass Company. The region's labour movement, however, did not exhibit comparable growth.

# Unemployment and Organization During the Great Depression

The years of the Great Depression were not auspicious for labour organizing. Given the high rates of unemployment, if workers protested too much, employers could easily replace them. But while thousands of Niagara workers lost their jobs from 1929 onward, not all sectors of the local economy were affected equally or at the same time. Some local industries expanded their facilities and workforces, and many employers used the depression to cut wages, speed up work, and undermine organizational efforts.

Surprisingly, despite the vulnerability of workers in a depressed economy, considerable labour protest and organizing took place in Niagara communities. Liberal Premier Mitchell Hepburn and his supporters were convinced that communist agitators were responsible for the unrest in the region. In particular, they saw communists behind the inroads that industrial unions connected to the

Congress of Industrial Organizations (CIO) were making in Niagara.[1] Unlike the craft unions affiliated with the American Federation of Labor, industrial unions belonging to the CIO organized all workers — regardless of craft or level of skill. Communist organizers interested in expanding their influence in Canada were, in fact, active in promoting such unions in Niagara. Contrary to Hepburn's allegations, however, the sources and goals of labour protest during the Great Depression were far too complex to be ascribed to communist organizing. The communists were able to garner support in the region in large measure because of the area's ethnic diversity. Ukrainian, Hungarian, and Croatian immigrants had established pro-communist associations in the area earlier in the century.

Although blaming communists for labour protest suited the purposes of Hepburn and local employers, only a minority of the protesters belonged to the Communist Party of Canada. Many of them supported the Co-operative Commonwealth Federation (CCF), a party strongly committed to parliamentary democracy. Unprecedented economic hardship and unemployment during the 1930s convinced many workers that the established political parties did not represent their interests. They were looking for new avenues that would permit them to participate in reshaping Canadian institutions to reflect working-class interests. Moreover, many Niagara workers who identified neither with the Communist Party nor with the CCF instead backed left-wing initiatives connected to unemployment relief and labour organizing. The gains that the CIO was making among workers in mass production industries in the United States undoubtedly added to the labour movement's appeal north of the border. Finally, the presence of experienced communist organizers also contributed to the revival of labour activism. For example, among Canadian political and labour groups, only the communists actively sought to organize the most vulnerable members of the working class: the unemployed. With their help, Niagara's unemployed protested against their predicament through demonstrations and strikes in a number of communities: Niagara Falls in 1934, Crowland in 1935, Thorold in 1936, and St. Catharines in 1937.[2]

# The Crowland Relief Strike

The longest of these strikes — and consequently the best documented — was the Crowland relief strike of 1935. Registered families in Crowland received relief in the form of food, clothing, shelter, and medical aid. In exchange, male family heads worked building sewers for the town. On 2 April 1935, upon learning that they would have to work longer hours for relief, the men laid down their tools. To understand why they resorted to striking, it is necessary to consider the situation of Crowland's unemployed in the years leading up to the strike. Communist organizers had participated in the formation of the Crowland Unemployed Association in 1932.[1] Local and provincial authorities tried to discredit the association's demands by blaming outside agitators for riling up the unemployed. In fact, however, the local unemployed had their own reasons for uniting in the Crowland Unemployed Association: first, because relief allotments were insufficient to support their families; second, because relief was denied to the unemployed who were single; and, third and more generally, because the system of relief in their community and elsewhere in Canada denied their basic rights and dignity. Relief allowances were intentionally kept low for fear that the "irresponsible" relief workers might lose their incentive to work if they received more generous aid. In addition, payment was made in vouchers rather than cash, to prevent recipients from spending their relief allotments on alcohol instead of providing food and other necessities for their families.

During the three years leading up to the strike, Crowland's unemployed and their supporters held meetings to discuss their grievances and demonstrations to publicize them. They also attempted to negotiate with local authorities. Crowland Council responded by prohibiting parades and banning the posting of signs and the distribution of handbills without police permission. The council also announced that if a relief recipient participated in such agitation, his entire family would be denied relief.[2] Convinced that no local politician represented their interests, the unemployed and their allies fielded their own slate of candidates in the township's elections of 1934–35.[3] Although these candidates were not elected, they enjoyed broad support in the polling subdivisions where foreign-born residents dominated. Within this context, in April 1935 the township council announced it would increase the hours of work required to earn relief.[4] Since recipients already deemed their allotments insufficient, they concluded that striking remained their only option. The Crowland Council retaliated by ending relief assistance for the strikers and their families.

In response, the strikers, their families, and their community supporters — men, women, and children — surrounded the relief office to force Crowland Council to meet with the strikers' delegates. When it became clear that the council would not consent to meet them, some of the strikers tried to force their way into the office, arguing that, as a public building, it could not be closed to them. The police also responded with force, assaulting some of the protesters and throwing tear gas into the crowd. The demonstrators dispersed quickly, but not before some of them vented their frustration by breaking the relief office windows.[5] That night the police arrested the strike's alleged leaders.[6]

The strikers did not give in. With their families and other supporters, they picketed the sewer project where they had worked and paraded through urban Crowland to demonstrate community solidarity. Crowland's reeve attempted to lure them back to work by promising that any striker who showed "a willingness to work" would be given a relief voucher, and he posted seventeen policemen by the sewer to guarantee protection to those who complied. But the crowd remained defiant. Women and children booed and derided the police and the public works foreman, even pelting them with dirt. "I had a glass of water for breakfast," shouted one woman in response to the foreman's suggestion that the strikers return to work. "What did you have — nice bread and butter?" "How can we work?" cried another, "We got no shoes or stockings or food." Acknowledging that they were hungry, they still insisted that there were no scabs among them.[7] Food and used clothing donated by neighbours, sympathetic local merchants, farmers, and workers from outside Crowland helped the strikers stand their ground. The Crowland Unemployed Association pointed to community support for the strikers to counter claims that outside agitators caused the strike:

> The solidarity of all the unemployed in this strike, irrespective of their different nationalities, religions, political viewpoints, completely discredits statements that the strike is caused by a few agitators and that they are leading the strike of unemployed merely for the sake of striking. Men, women and children do not parade the streets every day because they like it. Nor do they face tear gas, clubs and midnight arrests merely to cause trouble.[8]

Indeed, the relief strike was a remarkable example of the sense of solidarity that Crowland's ethnically diverse population of workers — employed and unemployed — had attained. Through their daily experiences in the small urban community's multiethnic "foreign" quarter, and on various jobs, they had become acutely conscious of their shared predicament as immigrants and workers.

Feeling helpless in the face of the strikers' determination, township officials sought Premier Hepburn's intervention. The premier was determined to make an example of the Crowland relief strikers so that their protest would not spread to other communities. He sent the Ontario Provincial Police to Crowland and visited the township himself, declaring that if the strikers refused to return to work, it would be a "battle to the bitter end."[9] Ultimately, concerted action on the part of local and provincial authorities succeeded in breaking the strikers' resolve. Welland County's crown attorney denied bail to two jailed strike leaders.[10] Another leader suddenly became the chief advocate of a return to work after he received a job offer thanks to Hepburn's influence.[11] Crowland Council made modest concessions to the strikers, announcing that although relief would still be given in the form of vouchers, their value would be increased and the vouchers broken into dollar units so that they could be used in different stores. Some of the strikers decided to return to work, and the strike petered out.[12] But even though the gains they made were minimal, the strikers' ability to transcend divisions based on ethnicity and to hold out for a month after they were cut off relief despite the forces aligned against them was impressive. The strike indicates that ethnic diversity was not necessarily an obstacle to working-class militancy. Rather, it could foster and aid workers' activism. In subsequent decades, Crowland's ethnically diverse workers would constitute a key source of union power in Niagara.

# The Cotton Mill Strike, 1936–37

A strike at Empire Cotton Mills, in Welland — one of the longest Depression-era strikes by Niagara workers who managed to hold on to their jobs — demonstrated similar interethnic solidarity. On 22 December 1935, 865 textile workers, consisting of 562 men and 303 women, walked off the job and stayed out for forty-two cold winter days.[1] Among them were French Canadians, Italians, Hungarians, Poles, and Ukrainians who protested against a succession of wage cuts and speed-ups that prevented them from earning enough to support themselves and their families despite working sixty hours a week. The strikers demanded a return to pre-Depression wage levels, shorter hours, union recognition, better quality cotton to work with, and proper ventilation in the mill, as many mill hands suffered from respiratory ailments. They also insisted that there be no discrimination against workers who supported the strike.

The cotton mill was one of the most notorious employers in Welland. Its employees worked longer hours for lower wages than any other workers in the city. Some of the workers lived in company housing — especially the French Canadians, who had been brought to Welland by the company from Montmorency, Québec. According to Welland's relief officer, once the rent was deducted from their wages, they were often left with no means of subsistence.[2] They were thus forced to apply to the city for relief. So unrewarding and unhealthy were conditions in the cotton mill that working-class parents in Welland sometimes used the threat of mill employment to convince their children to stay in school.[3] Yet, during the Depression, the cotton mill was the only employer hiring in the city. The mill was also the main local employer of women. Given the dearth of employment opportunities, workers could not be selective about where they worked.

The frustration of mill operatives was exacerbated a few years before the strike, when the company used the introduction of new machines as a reason to redesignate a large proportion of workers as "learners," who could be paid lower wages.[4] Claims that the new machines were more efficient than the old ones also justified an increase in the number of weaving frames each worker operated. These new demands were so great that, according to the company's own statement, only 40 percent of the learners on the new machines were able to meet them.[5] Management saw their failure not as indicative of unreasonable expectations but as evidence of its magnanimity: "We are obliged to pay learners though they are non-producers. It is really a case where they are being paid for going to school."[6] As piece workers, that is, as workers paid not by the hour but according to the amount they produced, even those with plenty of experience who managed to operate all the machines saw their income decline. This occurred both because of the company's increased expectations and because the quality of the cotton used was so poor that it kept breaking.

The strike began spontaneously with the walkout of night workers.[7] Alex Welch, an organizer for United Textile Workers of America (UTWA), arrived in town shortly thereafter, and the majority of the workers signed union cards. They demanded shorter hours, higher wages, and the right to be represented by UTWA.

In the beginning, the strikers' morale was high. Considering the group's ethnic diversity, their unity was as impressive as that of the Crowland relief strikers. They met in different ethnic community halls. Speeches and leaflets were translated into French, Hungarian, Italian, and Ukrainian. The strikers sang songs and huddled around fires in makeshift stoves to keep warm. They were militant, but they kept strict discipline to prevent violence and to demonstrate their respectability. The strike committee appointed two men on each picket shift to maintain order. Their bulletin announced that drunkenness on the picket line would not be tolerated. Women were asked to arrange shifts so that they would not have to be on the picket line between 11:00 p.m. and 5:00 a.m.[8] Only twice did strikers resort to violence. In one case, a group of strikers attacked "Red" Robinson, who was leading a group of workers to a storefront leased by the company to register their desire to return to work.[9] In the second case, seventy-year-old "Granny" Beaulieu attacked one of the foremen. She was out on the picket line to support her striking son, daughter, and fifteen-year old grandchild when she noticed the foreman trying to sneak into the plant. To stop him, Granny Beaulieu lunged at him and sent him staggering. Moments later, three policemen came to the foreman's rescue, but not before he "shrieked," to the great amusement of the picketers, "Arrest that woman! She attacked me!"[10]

Granny Beaulieu was not the only militant woman among the strikers. Mary Jary, a Saskatchewan-born daughter of Hungarian immigrants, was probably the most vocal and memorable of the strike committee members. Both she and her husband, George, a weaver from Hungary, worked at the cotton mill, but their wages were barely sufficient to support themselves and their young son. Despite the fact that women earned significantly less than men in the mill, she saw the strike in family, not gendered, terms. "If I died, my husband would have to get another woman to help him make a living," she explained.[11] But her acceptance of some prevailing gender norms did not extend to "ladylike" behaviour. As a native speaker of English, she was chosen as a spokesperson by the strikers. "What do you think of our spirit now?" she asked journalists covering the strike. "Haven't we got the light of battle in our eyes?"[12] Angrily rejecting the company's claims that "outside agitators" were responsible for the strike, Jary declared that the strike "had been forced on the employees by being forced down and then being stepped upon." Although union organizers were not responsible for initiating the strike, she had no doubts about the advantages of union power for the workers:

> Why is it that textile companies are so afraid of unions? With a union when we return to work there will be no need to bring kegs of wine, cakes and chicken to the bosses. You won't have to be good looking to get a break. You won't have to listen to some of that awful language we hear in the mill. The union would give everyone a fair chance and they would receive treatment like humans, not cattle."[13]

Dubbed the "Pasionaria of Welland" by the communist press, after Dolores Ibárruri, the fiery communist leader of the Spanish Civil War, Jary travelled through southern Ontario to publicize the strikers' goals and raise support for them among organized workers.

Nelson Batchelder, general manager of Empire Cotton Mills, kept insisting that provincial policemen be called to Welland. According to him, there would be "loss of life if we don't get adequate police to stem the mob."[14] In fact, picketing remained orderly. The strikers also enjoyed broad support in and beyond Welland. Local merchants supplied them with food and heating materials. Ethnic organizations held fundraisers for the strikers. Organized workers throughout southern Ontario donated funds as well, and both CCF and communist activists spoke out in their support. O. C. Jennette, an industrial standards officer sent by Ontario's Department of Labour to investigate the situation in Welland, also sided with the strikers. He found the wages paid by Empire Cotton Mills shockingly low. Teenagers, working at the mill because the wages earned by their parents were insufficient to support their families, earned less than $8.00 for fifty-five hours a week. Jennette highlighted the case of Henri Dorval, aged fifteen:

> When I questioned this boy as to what would be the reason that he would have to go to work so young, he informed me as follows: that his [father is] employed as a roving pilot at $14.45 for a 55 hour week, from which $3.75 was deducted for house rent, and that his father had eight children, the oldest being himself and the youngest seven months, and gave me some of the following expenses which he was forced to pay to exist. His light bill for two months $2.89; his gas bill $2 per month; his grocery bill $13.50 for a week; and that his mother was sickly; his father had not been able to purchase an overcoat in the past eleven years and a suit in the past four years; his little sisters and brothers needed shoes and he himself had no overcoat.[15]

L. B. Spencer, a Welland lawyer, blamed what he called the "deplorable conditions" at Empire Cotton Mills on the general manager. According to Spencer, quite apart from the question of wages, Batchelder's treatment of his "help" tended to "undermine the whole fabric of democracy and the establishment of government by reason, and is a definite influence over the long range to communism or fascism."[16] These reports convinced David Croll, Ontario's minister of Labour, to speak in support of the strikers. Pointing to the company's pay sheets as proof of exploitation, he denounced the "shameless underpayment and brutal exploitation" of workers and declared: "If ever a company seems deliberately to ask for labor trouble it is the Empire Cotton Mills. I have every sympathy for the strikers."[17] Local MPP E. J. Anderson, a Conservative, reported to his Ottawa counterpart that the people of Welland considered the strikers' demands reasonable.[18] The city's welfare board provided relief for needy strikers despite company accusations that the board was being too sympathetic to the strikers.[19]

On 11 January 1937, Batchelder announced the indefinite closure of Empire Cotton Mills. Meanwhile, company representatives did everything in their power to break the strikers' ranks and convince some of them to return to work. The company placed advertisements in local newspapers, including foreign-language ones. One of these advised its employees that because the company would not recognize the "American" textile workers union, "possession of its membership card will not give you any right to negotiate with the company." As the ad went on to say, "It is not necessary for you to pay dues to any union in order to get a square deal from this Canadian-owned company."[20] Another ad called on all workers who wanted to return to work to send their names to the company, adding that if enough names were submitted the company would guarantee protection when they returned to the mill. Company agents visited workers' homes to entice them back to the mill with verbal assurances. The company's lawyer approached Father László Forgách, the priest serving Hungarian Roman Catholics in Welland, and offered to pay him one thousand dollars to persuade his striking parishioners to return to work. But if the lawyer was counting on Roman Catholic antagonism to radicalism to sway the priest, he miscalculated. Father Forgách turned him down. He believed that the "strikers had every reason in the world to go on strike. The wages they earned were outrageous."[21]

On 18 January 1937, the company presented new proposals to the strikers. It agreed to review the wages of the lowest-paid adult males and promised to increase wages in future if it could. However, the company refused to recognize the strike committee, claiming that it represented a minority of extremists. It also refused to recognize UTWA. The strikers voted on the company's offer by a secret ballot under the supervision of the Welland city clerk and O. C. Jennette of the Ontario Department of Labour. The offer was refused by 653 of those who voted, 130 accepted it, and 6 spoiled their ballots.[22] Company officials nevertheless insisted that the strike committee did not represent the majority of workers, most of whom, they claimed, wished to return to work but were prevented from doing so by intimidation. The strike continued.

Gradually, however, the company's intransigence and threats to close the plant weakened the strikers' resolve. On 8 February 1937, Batchelder finally agreed to the recommendations of Louis Fine, of the Ontario Department of Labour, to increase the wages of the lowest-paid employees, to establish shop committees to take up grievances with management, to recognize the right of employees to belong to any organization of their choosing, and to allow all former employees to return to work without discrimination. The next day the workers accepted the offer. Batchelder immediately reneged on his promise to reinstate all striking workers.[23] Father Forgách, who knew what hardship awaited unemployed workers, went to Batchelder and begged him to take back the strikers, but his efforts were unsuccessful. Many of the strike leaders were blacklisted and consequently could not find work in any plant in Welland.[24] Only a decade later, in November 1946, would cotton mill workers finally succeed in winning recognition of their right to be represented by UTWA Local 155.

# The Monarch Strike

In 1938, workers employed by the Monarch Knitting Company in St. Catharines also walked off the job. The 1936 Royal Commission established by the federal government to investigate conditions in the textile industry had already deemed that protest by textile workers was well warranted. It discovered, for example, that textile manufacturers were cutting wages, despite making healthy profits. As a result, the income of a growing proportion of textile workers, in St. Catharines and elsewhere, declined below the minimum required for survival.[1]

Monarch Knitting Company workers responded to wage cuts and speed-ups by organizing Local 5 of the Canadian Full-Fashioned Hosiery Workers' Association. The intense anti-unionism of

Niagara employers found expression in the testimony of J. A. Burns, president and general manager of the Monarch Knitting Company, before the Royal Commission on Textile Industries. He claimed that "agitators" sent from the United States were responsible for union organizing at Monarch. Their goal, he claimed, was to take workers' money in the form of union dues, and he warned that if such agitators did not succeed in fomenting strikes, they would not hesitate to leave town with the workers' funds. "They have not the employees at heart, they are thinking about their own welfare," Burns explained. He fired members of the shop committee, two of whom were women, and threatened to close the St. Catharines plant if labour unrest continued.[2]

Monarch Knitting Company, St. Catharines.
Courtesy of the St. Catharines Public Library, Special Collections.

But the Canadian Full-Fashioned Hosiery Workers' Association was — ironically, in view of Burns's claims — almost as critical of the CIO as Burns himself. The union belonged to the All-Canadian Congress of Labour, a small, nationalist labour federation that refused affiliation with American-led international unions. Its members rejected the tactics of the CIO as unduly radical, stressing instead their desire to cooperate with employers. The firing of their shop committee, however, made such cooperation impossible. Monarch workers walked out and stayed on strike for eleven weeks, demanding that the fired shop committee be reinstated. Hosiery workers from Hamilton, London, and Toronto supported the strikers and threatened a general strike in their trade. After both sides agreed to conciliation, the Industry and Labour Board instructed the company to rehire the two female shop committee members and to help its male head find another job.[3]

Another irony of this strike is that, despite the presence of women in its organizing campaigns, male organizers complained about the difficulty of convincing female employees of Monarch Knitting to join their union. Their complaints were probably not without foundation. While some women supported unions, many more did not. Monarch's male employees were quite wrong, however, to attribute the women's reluctance to timidity. Many of the women, who generally stayed in paid employment only until they married, were less committed to their jobs and hence to organizing than their male counterparts. Their low wages, even for performing the same jobs as men, contributed to their reluctance to stay in factories. Around the time of the strike at Monarch, where both men and women were employed as knitters, adult female knitters earned only 62 percent of the wages of adult males.[4] That their union took such unequal wages for granted probably did not help matters. Working women's household responsibilities also meant that they had less time and energy to devote to union activities than did male workers.

# The CIO at McKinnon Industries

Workers at McKinnon Industries did turn to the CIO in 1936, when they established Local 199 of the United Automobile Workers of America (UAW), the first CIO local in Niagara. McKinnon's was a locally owned manufacturer of buggy components that moved successfully into the production of motor vehicle parts in the early twentieth century and became a General Motors (GM) subsidiary in 1929. The company had established a workers' council, but workers who attempted to use it not simply as a forum for venting frustrations but also as a means to bring about meaningful change were disappointed. The company took no action in response to worker complaints. When the workers decided to join the UAW, they received assistance from experienced organizers, some of whom were also members of the Communist Party. But while the founding of Local 199 of the UAW, which would become the largest and most powerful union in St. Catharines, was clearly inspired by developments in the United States, the organizational initiative appears to have been wholly local.[1]

The provincial government, under the leadership of Premier Hepburn, whose opposition to the CIO in Oshawa and northern Ontario was well-known, shared the eagerness of management to oust the UAW from McKinnon. Hepburn sent in the provincial police, hoping that the organizing drive could be defeated by charging union activists with inciting unlawful behaviour. In an attempt to break worker solidarity, the police interviewed workers in their homes, but they were unable to obtain information that would have allowed them to lay charges against anyone.[2]

The *St. Catharines Standard* sided with Hepburn and McKinnon Industries. The paper described union organizers as "foreign agitators" whose ambition for power brought only "distress and misery" to the workers "whom they are able to exploit." The newspaper also lamented the "economic tragedy" resulting from the "war between capital and labor" instigated by sit-down strikes in the United States, adding that similar developments in St. Catharines would scare off prospective new industries. The paper did not hesitate to use both racism and sexism to discredit the UAW. When Sam Kraisman, the business agent of the CIO-affiliated International Ladies' Garment Workers' Union (ILGWU), came to speak to St. Catharines workers, the *Standard* asked rhetorically, "What have Toronto Jewish women's delegates with strike experience in the clothing trade to offer St. Catharines motor workers"?[3]

Most McKinnon workers belonging to ethnic minorities responded with enthusiasm to the industrial unionism of the CIO. A disproportionate number of them signed the UAW's first charter at the factory. As unskilled workers, they had not been eligible for membership in craft unions, and, being particularly vulnerable to dismissal, they generally feared to express grievances without an organization to defend their rights. Yet all of them knew someone who had been injured on the job, and since they had the dirtiest jobs at the plant, many of them suffered from diseases like silicosis. They resented the power and arbitrariness of foremen who expected personal favours from immigrant workers who wanted to get a job for a relative or friend, or a better job for themselves, or simply to keep their jobs during the Depression. Some supervisors pushed immigrant workers to bring them bottles of scotch or treat them to drinks after work, invite them home for dinner, clear their driveways in winter, or mow their lawns in summer. The immigrants were also angered by the company's discriminatory employment policies, which kept non–Anglo-Celtic workers out of skilled and white-collar jobs. Older immigrant workers, with little education and limited knowledge of English, were generally not in a position to aim for such jobs, but they held such hopes for their Canadian-educated children. Yet the daughter of Armenian immigrants recalled:

No Armenian women were hired as clerical help. . . . It was hard for foreign women to get in the office at McKinnon's. A man by the name of McCarthy ran the office and he didn't like foreigners. . . . I also applied for a job in Fleming's [law firm] office but I knew they wouldn't hire us because we were Armenian. So I worked in the factory and then got married. I'm sure my qualifications were fine.[4]

Meanwhile, the UAW went out of its way to appeal to minority workers. To convey its message, it arranged for interpreters for those workers who had a limited grasp of English. In contrast to the company's policy of excluding "foreigners" from white-collar jobs, the union provided opportunities for advancement to talented members of minority groups. Armenian Canadian Hygus Torosian, for example, a founding member of Local 199 of the UAW and one of the most active members of the local's educational committee, was awarded a scholarship to study at the Workers' Educational Association Training School in England so that he could equip himself "for even more effective work in his organization and community."[5]

In May 1937, McKinnon workers gave their overwhelming support to the UAW when 1,190 workers voted to join the union. Only twelve workers opposed the move.

# Fighting for Democracy
# on the Home Front, 1939–45

During the war, when serious labour shortages developed, workers were again in a strong position to promote their interests. Men and increasingly women as well joined unions and demanded higher wages, the right to organize, and worker representation on government boards. McKinnon workers were no exception. In 1941, when they struck for higher wages and the right to organize, they justified their demands not simply in terms of need but also on the grounds of equity. They maintained that while workers were being pressured to work harder and faster for patriotic reasons, employers were profiting from war.

McKinnon Industries responded by intensifying its anti-union campaign. Management fomented suspicion of "foreign" workers, both because employers often saw immigrant workers as radicals and because management believed that pointing to immigrants' role in the UAW would create divisions among workers. The company's hiring policies indicated its distrust of non–Anglo-Celtic workers. When it requested machinists trained by the Dominion Provincial Wartime Emergency Training Programme, it specified that such men should be between the ages of twenty-six and forty, should weigh at least 150 pounds, and should be "of Anglo Saxon origin if possible."

But the company also promoted suspicions toward non–Anglo-Celtic workers more actively. In a signed affidavit, Donald Schoures, a McKinnon worker, described the activities of Major Carmichael, also known as "Digger," another of the company's employees:

I, Donald Schoures, hereby testify to efforts by one known to me as Digger in attempting to form a secret organization of employees of the McKinnon Industries Limited, St. Catharines. Early in Sept. 1941, I was approached by a group leader in the plant, Arthur Othen, and requested if I wished to attend a meeting on government business. I was taken to a meeting of other McKinnon Group leaders and employees of the Co., employees who had attended upon the invitation of various group leaders. The person known as Digger but has been identified as one Colonel Carmichael was the leader and principle [sic] speaker. The people present at the meeting were informed by Digger that they were there to combat any forms of sabotage. In his speech the speaker advised all present to watch the McKinnon employees of foreign extraction while in the plant for possible sabotage by them. The Digger stated he was in favour of unions but that Local 199 UAW-CIO was dominated by foreign born people and the leaders of the union would be guilty of sabotage if strike action took place at the McKinnon plant. He requested all members of his organization the Inner Circle Counter-Sabotage Committee to keep the wheels of industry turning whatever the cost. Included in the membership of the Inner Circle Counter Sabotage Committee were members of Local 199 UAW-CIO. Statements made by Digger at this meeting proved he was in receipt of decisions made at union meetings. He condemned the union in the taking of the strike ballot declaring it was not properly conducted, members being forced to vote in favour of strike action which was untrue. He further declared any strike action would be illegal which was untrue. Throughout the meeting he dwelt on the functions of the union which he criticized, rather than forms of sabotage the organization he had set up was supposed to discuss. In my opinion the Inner Circle Counter Sabotage Committee was set up as an anti-union organization rather than an anti-sabotage group.[1]

In the name of patriotism, the federal and provincial governments and the mainstream local press sided with management against the union. In a radio address, C. D. Howe, Canada's powerful federal minister of Munitions and Supply, urged St. Catharines workers to keep working. He sent two hundred RCMP officers to St. Catharines, claiming that they were needed to ensure that those who wanted to keep working would not be harassed by picketers, despite the fact that local police reported that picketing was peaceful. Premier Hepburn described the strikers as "just as big an enemy as the Germans."[2] The *St. Catharines Standard* backed the government. "Every hour of the strike here," one of its editorials stated, "helps the dastardly beast, Hitler." The editorial worried that striking workers would tarnish the image of all St. Catharines workers by showing that they were more concerned with "a few cents more an hour" than they were "to do their bit to help humanity."[3] The *Standard* did not mention that McKinnon workers were earning less than autoworkers in Oshawa and Windsor. Instead, it denounced them for being unpatriotic and selfish and for causing layoffs in other plants.

Most striking workers did not lose their determination in the face of such opposition. They had no doubts about the importance of their contribution to the war effort. As "Just Another Worker" wrote to the *Standard*, when the government declared its plans to cap profits, manufacturers "went on strike," claiming that they would not make enough profits. The government altered its plans in response. The absence of labour representation on any war boards no doubt helped. "Why can't we have decent men in Ottawa," the worker asked, "instead of having a group of Canadian Manufacturers' Association puppets who are always thinking in terms of profits rather than sacrificing?"[4]

Women, who entered factories such as McKinnon in growing numbers, were among the most outspoken defenders of the strike. One "girl employee" wrote to the *St. Catharines Standard:*

I am not so good at composing a letter of this kind, but I believe I can convey my meaning. I am one of the girl employees on strike at McKinnons'. I have worked there a good number of years and every time I have ever asked for a raise, have been told the company could not afford it. . . . As for being patriotic, I have a kid brother overseas and I certainly would like to see a decent set wage for him to come back to. He quit McKinnons on account of receiving 25¢ per hour. . . . If the so-called big names feel they would like to sacrifice and be patriotic, they can take their own sons and daughters out of college and let them do their share of slaving. McKinnons and the government have their representatives and we picked Bob Stacey as ours. As far as I know I certainly was not forced or coerced into joining the union. I joined because it stands for democracy, which is what we are trying to fight for. There are plenty of millionaires being made out of this war and they sure do not care who gives their lives as long as they rake in the money. We don't want Hitler here, but we are being run by a few "would-be" Hitlers. The working man of McKinnons should be able to live not merely exist and have the right to save a dollar and send their children to college the same as G.M.'s executives do. The workers are the ones that count and should not be treated as ignorant dogs. If I did not have my parents to live with I would have gone short many a day on McKinnons' pay. . . . Here's hoping the government realizes we have to live too![5]

That this young woman understood her low wages and general inequality solely in terms of class, and not gender, tells us a great deal about widespread acceptance of gender inequality even among workers, including militant female workers.

Women war workers making munitions at McKinnon Industries.
Courtesy of the *St. Catharines Standard.*

The strike was well organized and peaceful. A female picketer brought a "camera-type" radio to the picket line. Girls and youths distributed song sheets and harmonized strike songs and "current tunes" as they walked the line, at times accompanied by a mouth-organ playing picketer.[6] The workers' relaxed approach reflected not only their position of relative strength in the context of serious labour shortages but also their refusal to see a contradiction between their rights to organize and receive fair wages and their loyalty to Canada and the war effort. The "democratic Canada" they hoped to establish as workers on the home front would clearly offer equal opportunities for the members of all classes.

The strikers' views were shared by workers throughout Canada and by a large segment of the local community. The St. Catharines Trades and Labour Council, the Canadian Congress of Labour (CCL, founded in 1940 as a merger of the All-Canadian Congress of Labour and the Canadian branch of the CIO), the Toronto Trades and Labour Council (affiliated with the AFL), the Toronto Labour Council (affiliated with the CCL), the Montreal Labour Council, and workers from Halifax, Sydney, Winnipeg, and Port Arthur sent messages of support. About sixty workers belonging to unions ranging from Cape Breton miners to the International Woodworkers of America (IWA) in British Columbia came down from nearby Hamilton, where the CCL was holding its annual convention, to join the picket lines.[7] To feed the strikers, local farmers donated fruits and vegetables, merchants gave other food items, and restaurants sent food to the kitchen run by Local 199's women's auxiliary. The strike ended when the company agreed to a closed shop and to negotiate wages.

Fomenting ethnic discord was not the only anti-union tactic on which Niagara employers relied during the Second World War. Throughout the peninsula, employers who had learned that their workers were in the process of organizing made a point of promoting company unions, which had no affiliation with the broader labour movement. Such campaigns against industrial unions were very much in evidence in Welland in 1942, when the United Electrical, Radio and Machine Workers Union (UE) was making inroads in several plants. Management at the Electro-Metallurgical plant called together representatives from each department and showed them a wide range of possible contracts it was willing to sign provided they formed a company, or "independent," union. The workers rejected this offer and were the first group in Welland to join the UE. The president of the UE, C. S. Jackson, recalled that when he arrived in Welland to help with the Electro-Metallurgical organizing drive he found that it actually required little input from him, as rank-and-file enthusiasm propelled the drive. So many people had come to a meeting at the Welland Hungarian Hall that Jackson had to fight his way inside. When he finally got to the front, he realized that "there was no point in wasting time." He gave a five-minute speech and started handing out membership cards. "The demands for the cards were coming from outside as well as inside the hall. Cards were going across this way and coming back with two dollars attached to them." That night, when the union's treasury contained a mere fifty dollars, Jackson took in between $700 and $800 in initiation fees.[8]

Mike Bosnich, a Welland worker of Croatian origin and later the UE's local business agent, ascribed the union's tremendous success at its inception to support from immigrant workers. They supported the union because it "overrode nationalities," enabling immigrant workers "to have a say in their wages, working conditions, and have some modicum of control over their futures" and ultimately to avoid "the discrimination that existed for many years, to manage to build job security." For them, the union was an organization "that was long overdue — that would give them the chance for self-respect and decency." That, Bosnich believed, "was more important to them than even the money or the union security."[9]

But unions did not always succeed in defeating company initiatives. In Welland, the Atlas Steels Employees' Association, which had been responsible for social and recreational activities among the workers since 1935, transformed itself into the Atlas Workers' Independent Union by issuing a new constitution in 1942 that empowered the association to bargain collectively with their employer. While the Independent Union claimed to have been formed by "the more stable and highly skilled operators and mechanics in the plant of Atlas Steels . . . entirely on their own initiative," the records of the UE attribute the initiative for its formation to the employer. Support for the UE among Atlas workers came from the semi-skilled and unskilled, who challenged the Independent Union's right to represent them and called in officials from the Department of Labour to oversee a vote by the workers. In a process deemed fair by the department officials, 1,263 workers supported the UE, and only 110 voted against. The company, however, refused to recognize the UE as the bargaining agent for Atlas workers. Instead, it signed a contract with the Atlas Workers' Independent Union and conducted a vote on that contract. The company could disregard its workers' decision with such impunity because, although the wartime government recognized the right of workers to be represented by a union of their choice, it did not compel employers to negotiate with such unions. Frustrated by the company's blatant disregard for the democratic process, the UE urged its supporters to boycott the vote, and the new contract was approved by only a narrow majority. Despite the company's failure to respect the initial vote, Ontario's labour court validated the contract with the company union.[10]

Other companies adopted similar tactics. North American Cyanamid, the largest employer in Niagara Falls, responded to an organizing drive by the United Gas, Coke and Chemical Workers of America in 1943 by drafting a Company Union Agreement and getting its employees' Improvement and Development Committee, renamed the General Plant Committee, to sign the document. According to Cyanamid workers, the agreement, "which was signed and then revised by the Company," was not submitted to the employees for ratification. Nor were the employees ever asked whether "they wanted this agreement or even wanted this committee to act on their behalf on such matters."[11] The Welland Chemical Works, a crown corporation operating under Cyanamid management during the war, similarly designated an employee association to represent its workers and refused to negotiate with the CIO.[12]

Despite these anti-union efforts, Niagara workers joined industrial unions in growing numbers and fought for higher wages and better conditions. Their ranks included seasonal agricultural labourers and workers in canneries and in the service industries, all of whom had historically found it difficult to organize. In 1941, striking McKinnon workers helped increase the wages of agricultural workers. Excused from strike duty, automotive workers from low-wage groups picked peaches for local farmers desperately short of workers. They used their experience in the labour movement to win an extra five cents per hour of picking. Women employed by Canadian Canners struck for and won higher wages and better working conditions at the Niagara-on-the-Lake plant.[13] Waiters and waitresses at the General Brock Hotel, walking out when two of their ranks were fired, demanded that management recognize their union, Local 299 of the International Hotel and Restaurant Employees' Union.[14]

Crowland-Welland and the UE constituted the nucleus of Niagara's labour movement, largely because of the ethnic make-up of these communities. Crowland, in particular, had a much higher percentage of non–Anglo-Celtic residents than any other community in the region — or, for that matter, anywhere else in Ontario except in northern resource communities. The township's small size prevented the emergence of exclusive ethnic enclaves among these residents, most of whom belonged to the working class. As the actions of Crowland's unemployed demonstrated, daily contact across ethnic lines in Crowland's foreign quarter and in semi-skilled and unskilled jobs in factories and on construction sites contributed to an awareness of shared grievances and goals among minority workers. The strongest integrative force among them, however, was the discrimination they all faced.

The particular ethnic mix of these workers helps to explain their militancy. Radical Ukrainians, Hungarians, Croatians, and Serbians — the members of ethnic groups with strong communist-led factions in Canada — played a key role in the wartime and postwar unionization drives in Crowland, in Welland, and beyond. Many immigrant workers who were not themselves communists accepted their leadership, because local communists seemed to be the most committed and capable advocates of their cause.

The UE's efforts to extend union power beyond the shop floor appealed to Crowland and Welland workers, whatever their ideological inclinations. In Crowland, UE activists were regularly elected to Crowland Council, where they fought to extend better municipal services to workers and to pay for them by ending tax exemptions and free services for the large companies within the township. The UE also created a twentieth-century version of the type of working-class culture the Knights of Labor had created in Niagara in the nineteenth century. It hosted social occasions such as picnics, excursions, dinners, and Christmas parties for its members and their families, sponsored local baseball and hockey teams, and supported local charities such as the Red Cross, the Salvation Army, and a children's shelter.[15]

But despite the growth of union power, the limits to labour's ethnic inclusiveness in Niagara persisted. McKinnon workers, for example, had no qualms about protesting against the hiring of Japanese Canadians. As a result, the Japanese Canadians who were relocated by the government to this area were largely confined to low-paying, labour-intensive jobs in agriculture and in canneries and basket factories. Discrimination against them continued after the war as well. Harry Kurahara recalled attempting to move from a basket-making factory in Grimsby to McKinnon Industries in 1948:

> I went to McKinnon in 1948 to put my name in, and the guy said they were not hiring, just like that. But you know, the same afternoon two young fellows I knew went and got jobs with McKinnon. From that day on I thought that guy was a redneck, he doesn't like Japanese otherwise why would he say they weren't hiring and turn around and hire two guys? So from that day on, me and General Motors, we don't agree, from that day on I wouldn't buy a GM product. It hurt, but you convince yourself you're as good as that guy.[16]

Union organizers showed greater awareness that their own failure to defend women's interests may have contributed to the union's weakness among female workers at McKinnon Industries. During a discussion of problems facing Local 199 at a meeting of the District Council of the UAW in June 1942, they explained: "We will remain weak with [women] unless we can lead the way on equal pay for equal work." But despite the presence of such militant and clear-sighted female workers at the plant as the "girl employee" who wrote to the *St. Catharines Standard*, Local 199 representatives still maintained that it was "hard to find people with leadership potential among the girls themselves."[17]

Meanwhile, the strength of working-class discontent, expressed by a large number of strikes as well as CCF electoral gains, convinced the provincial government that it might have to recognize workers' right to collective bargaining. In 1943, the provincially appointed Select Committee to Inquire into Collective Bargaining Between Employers and Employees invited testimony from Ontario workers and employers. The large delegations from Niagara reflected how polarized the area was along class lines. The largest local employers were represented: McKinnon Industries, Lightning Fastener, English Electric, Hayes Steel, Imperial Iron, McKinnon Columbus Chain, Packard Electric, St. Catharines Steel Products, Thompson Products, Welland Vale, Engineering Tool and Forgings, and the Foster Wheeler Corporation, all from St. Catharines; from Welland, Atlas Steels; from Niagara Falls, North American Cyanamid; from Port Colborne, Canadian Furnace; from Thorold, the Ontario Paper Company; and from Merriton, the Alliance Paper Company. These companies had organized a year earlier as a non-profit corporation named the Niagara Industrial Relations Institute, proclaiming their desire "to improve industrial relations between employers and employees in the Niagara peninsula and to formulate policies for proper collective bargaining relations between employers and employees in that district." In fact, the brief presented to the Select Committee by their lawyer, J. L. Gabriel Keogh, made clear that the Niagara Industrial Relations Institute wanted to protect company unions and to limit the power of the industrial unions that had succeeded in gaining a foothold in the area.

In this confrontation, the well-represented workers and other supporters of collective bargaining were still unable to carry the day. The Ontario government listened to their accounts of employers throughout the peninsula forcing (and sometimes bribing) workers to support employee associations that purported to be independent but were, for all intents and purposes, not much different from company unions. The government apparently accepted labour's claim that the overwhelming majority of workers in the area supported labour unions and wanted state recognition of their right to collective bargaining, but it was ultimately unwilling to ban the formation of "independent" company unions as part of the 1943 Ontario Collective Bargaining Act. Employers continued to use company unions to block the organization of affiliated unions for decades to come.[18]

# Niagara Labour's Cold War

For Canadian and Niagara workers, the fight to establish their right to collective bargaining represented by a union of their choice did not end with the war. At this time, shop stewards collected union dues to secure membership stability on a monthly basis. Considerable labour turnover made this difficult even during the war. With the prospect of the type of economic recession that followed the First World War threatening to undermine their bargaining position, union officials feared that the existence of unions would again become precarious once war production ended. Pointing to the indispensable part that labour had played in the war effort, union supporters demanded legal protections. To gain financial stability, they sought compulsory dues check-offs from workers' pay cheques. To guarantee membership stability, they wanted the closed shop — compulsory membership in the union — in all unionized workplaces. Moreover, having accepted caps on wages throughout the war, workers now demanded increases. A wave of strikes throughout the country, most famously by Ford workers at Windsor, forced the federal government to concede to some union demands. The Rand formula (1946), proposed by Supreme Court Justice Ivan Rand, was founded on the recognition of unequal power between employers and workers. Justice Rand believed that a legislated dues check-off would redress the balance by strengthening the position of unions vis-à-vis employers. The Rand formula did not establish the closed shop, because Justice Rand believed that complusory union membership infringed on the individual rights of workers. But it did require all workers — even those who did not want to join unions — to pay union dues on the grounds that they benefitted from union representation.

Even this new postwar legality did not, however, put an end to employers' campaigns against unions affiliated with the wider labour movement. Company unions remained key components of these campaigns. Amidst the vehement anti-communism of the Cold War years, red-baiting also became a strong feature of the postwar anti-union campaign.

The short-lived success of the AFL-affiliated United Textile Workers of America at Welland's Plymouth Cordage Company in 1948–49 illustrates how employers used both company unions and red-baiting to combat the organized labour movement. During the years of World War II, the company had again been forced to recruit new workers, mostly women and racialized Chinese, as it had done during World War I. The company's welfare plan had proved insufficient to counter the lure of higher wages offered by other wartime employers in Welland, and many workers had expressed their discontent with Plymouth Cordage by leaving. Not until 1948, however, did Cordage workers choose to buttress their position by forming Local 174 of UTWA. Both the growing number of younger workers at the Cordage factory and a strong campaign by the union, which had built a foundation in Welland in 1936–37 by organizing workers at Empire Cotton Mills, were responsible for UTWA's gaining a foothold at Plymouth Cordage. Yet, after the first contract expired, a majority of Cordage workers voted to return to their employee association. What explains this about-face?

That the experiment with the international union was short-lived can be attributed to a number of factors. Most importantly, when the contract with UTWA ended, the company laid off about a hundred younger workers, some of whom were union activists. In contrast, to judge from the leadership of the employee association, its base of support lay among older employees, who, with some reservations, continued to see the Plymouth Cordage Company as a "good employer." Moreover, on the eve of the vote to choose a union to represent them, workers were offered the opportunity to buy lots from the company at advantageous prices. As the cartoon below suggests, the company also conducted a campaign to discredit the union on the grounds of its communist leadership. Finally, and somewhat ironically, in part because of the competition from UTWA and other unions eager to represent Cordage workers, the employee association had some success in obtaining better terms for its members.[1]

Cartoon from a Plymouth Cordage Employee Association publication, 1949. Courtesy of Library and Archives Canada (Madeleine Parent and R. Kent Rowley fonds).

A similar contest took place between a company union and the United Electrical, Radio and Machine Workers Union at the American Cyanamid Company in Niagara Falls. The Cyanamid Independent Union, established in 1943, represented the workers until 1953, when the UE conducted a successful organizing drive at the plant.[2] Cyanamid workers went out on strike six months later, when the union and the company failed to reach agreement on the initial contract. This was the first strike in the company's forty-five years of operations in Niagara Falls. Both the company and the union valued and worked hard to win community support. Both camps purchased centrefold advertisements in the Niagara Falls *Evening Review* to present their side of the dispute. The company declared that, until union supporters demonstrated a willingness to conduct themselves in "a responsible manner," it would not contribute to union security in the form of a dues check-off and a closed shop. It also claimed that union security and control over grievances would not benefit Cyanamid employees; rather, only the UE stood to benefit. The company reminded Niagara Falls residents of its standing in the community as one of the foremost employers for forty-five years and stressed its commitment to progressive employer-employee relations, as evidenced by its ongoing concerns about working conditions, health, and safety and its insurance and pension plans. It accused the UE of "fantastic" and "impossible" economic demands, "devious purposes" in entrenching itself not only at the Cyanamid plant but in the wider community, and of establishing "a beachhead" in the chemical industry in Canada. Cyanamid declared its empathy with workers' families and local businesses for the economic losses they would suffer because of the strike. As a *coup de grâce,* it closed the company swimming pool — the only public pool in Niagara Falls — on the grounds that picketing threatened the safety of anyone wishing to enter company grounds. "One does not invite guests to one's home," it declared in a large advertisement in the Niagara Falls paper, "when the possibility of embarrassment and the threat of bodily harm are present."[3]

The UE, for its part, levelled various charges against the Cyanamid Corporation, not least that it had benefitted greatly from tax breaks. Despite these advantages and its considerable profits, it refused realistic wage increases. The company's demands concerning management control were unreasonable, as it wanted to allow foremen to decide whether workers were performing adequately without permitting workers to file a grievance if they were disciplined. The UE also condemned Cyanamid for refusing to conform to the practices of other employers in Niagara who followed the recommendations of conciliation boards concerning wage increases and seniority rights.[4]

American Cyanamid Company swimming pool, August 1941.
Courtesy of the Niagara Falls (Ontario) Public Library (D414251).

The Cold War was fought not only between employers and workers in Niagara but also within unions. Here, as elsewhere in Canada, the conflict within the labour movement concerned partisan politics. Having witnessed the success of the social-democratic CCF in federal and provincial elections, some labour leaders wanted to lend formal union support to the party. Communist labour activists, however, who did not themselves refrain from advocating union support for Communist Party candidates in ridings where they stood a chance of winning, recognized that communists enjoyed limited political support and therefore called for union neutrality in elections. The split within Local 529 of the UE in St. Catharines offers a clear example of the fissures that politics created in the labour movement. The local represented workers at the English Electric and the Yale and Towne companies. CCF supporters began their campaign by trying to oust communists from the local's leadership.

American Cyanamid Company swimming pool high diving boards, circa 1940s.
Courtesy of the Niagara Falls (Ontario) Public Library (D421215F).

Workers sympathetic to the Communist Party accused those who
called for closer ties with the CCF of injecting "narrow partisan

politics into the Local." Other members pointed out that all of the local's officers had been democratically elected and could therefore not be removed from their positions. Eventually the conflict led to the division of the local. English Electric workers left the UE to support the United Steelworkers of America (USWA), which had strong ties with the CCF. Yale and Towne workers remained within the UE. At the national level, the UE was expelled from the Canadian Congress of Labour, one of Canada's two large labour federations, thanks to pressure from the US-based CIO and from both conservative and CCF supporters within the labour movement in Canada, on the pretext that it had not paid its membership dues on time.[5]

All the same, anti-communist propaganda failed to persuade many of Niagara's workers. Electro-Metallurgical, Page-Hersey, Yale and Towne, and International Silver workers continued to adhere to the UE, even after the union was expelled from the CCL and despite raids from CCL unions, especially the USWA. Radical workers belonging to or sympathetic to the Communist Party remained active within UAW Locals in St. Catharines as well. Labour historians generally believe that politics was not, in fact, the main reason for workers' loyalty to the UE. Rather, workers remained loyal to the communist-led union because it was a "fighting union." The union's democratic structure and close ties to rank-and-file members were also important. In the ethnically diverse Niagara Peninsula, the ties between radical ethnic organizations and the UE were central to its success.

During the 1950s and 1960s, even non-unionized workers benefitted from the strength of the UE in the region. Employers in non-unionized plants such as Atlas Steels kept a close eye on the collective agreements signed by the UE and generally matched the wages and benefits they offered in order to keep the union out. Thanks to union power, by the mid-twentieth century Welland's workers were among the best paid in Canada. UE locals, along with other unions active in the area such as the UAW and USWA in St. Catharines and the Pulp and Paper Workers in Thorold, obtained advantageous contracts for their workers.

# Women and Workers of Colour
# in the 1950s and 1960s

The immediate postwar period was one of prosperity and growth in the Niagara area. As local industries switched back to manufacturing consumer goods, their labour needs were filled in part by new waves of immigrants from Britain and continental Europe. In these years, when so many workers enjoyed secure jobs and decent wages, the labour movement throughout Canada directed considerable energy to fighting racism through anti-discrimination legislation. Thanks in no small part to labour's efforts, starting in 1944 the Ontario government passed laws forbidding discrimination based on race, religion, colour, or nationality in public signs, employment, the provision of services, and the sale of property. No law, however, addressed discrimination in apartment rentals in the province.

A case of housing discrimination in St. Catharines in 1959 pushed the St. Catharines and District Labour Council to the centre of labour's fight against such discrimination. The case, covered by newspapers across the nation, involved a family of four by the name of Summers. Charles Summers, a truck driver, his pregnant wife, Ada, and their two young children were told to leave their apartment on Ontario Street because, as the *St. Catharines Standard* put it, "they were Negroes." They had been living in the apartment for a mere two months when, in September 1959, their landlady asked them to leave. She had received a number of anonymous letters from Ontario Street residents complaining that they did not want "colored people" living there.[1] A group signing itself as "McKinnon customers" sent a similar letter to Jack Woods, owner of the Coffizon, a restaurant located on Ontario Street near the McKinnon plant. Woods rented his premises from the owner of the building in which the Summers lived. His racist customers threatened to stop spending money in his restaurant unless he put pressure on his landlady to evict the Summers family.[2]

St. Catharines-born Ron Nicholson working at McKinnon Industries, 1951.
Courtesy of the St. Catharines Museum.

Charles Summers, a native of St. Catharines, refused to leave. When his landlady first approached him, he asked her for a written notice. Having obtained the documentation, he contacted the *St. Catharines Standard* to publicize this racist incident. "I felt that if I didn't take a stand now," he told the paper, "my children and in turn their children would have to face the same discrimination during their lives. I want this kind of thing to stop now."[3] Summers's stand encouraged African Canadians and other local residents to speak out against discrimination. Russell Thompson, a member of the Meliorist Club, an African Canadian service club, told reporters that up to 80 percent of young African Canadians in the area were unable to find work, that few barber shops in St. Catharines would serve African Canadians, and that there had been earlier attempts to prevent them from settling in certain parts of the city.[4]

The labour movement rallied behind Summers. Having received a number of complaints about similar discrimination in Toronto, the Toronto and District Labour Committee for Human Rights was campaigning to convince the Ontario government to pass legislation that would outlaw discrimination based on nationality, race, or religion in rental housing. However, they found it difficult to document specific cases of discrimination. Understandably, very few members of minority groups had the courage to publicize the humiliation that they suffered in their daily lives; some were even afraid that publicity would expose them to greater hostility. Consequently, when Charles Summers brought his experiences to the public's attention, the executive secretary of the Toronto and District Labour Committee for Human Rights, lawyer A. Alan Borovoy, took note of his courageous stand. Borovoy believed that if the St. Catharines City Council could be persuaded to pass a by-law against such discrimination, the provincial government would be more willing to pass anti-discrimination legislation. He contacted John Ideson, president of the St. Catharines and District Labour Council and a strong supporter of anti-discrimination legislation, and they worked together to prevent the eviction of the Summers family and to establish a deputation to the city council.[5]

Responses to this campaign suggest that, by the late 1950s, many residents of Niagara were upset by the open racism in the area. When Borovoy circulated a petition opposing the eviction of the Summers family, most of their neighbours on Ontario Street signed it. One of them, Mrs Kalagian, an Armenian Canadian, called on the family and said, "I want to tell you, you're the best people we have seen in ten years. . . . We want no part of this letter business."[6] Jack Wood of the Coffizon Restaurant angrily responded to racist customers who pressured him to urge the family's eviction: "I would rather go out of business than have a part in persecuting innocent people."[7] Letters of protest appeared in the *St. Catharines Standard*. Others expressed their support for the Summers family by telephone, and some even offered them alternative housing. A doctor from Niagara Falls sent money to help with a down payment on a house.[8] Newspaper coverage of the Summers case from places as distant as Sydney, Nova Scotia, suggest that many Canadians outside Niagara also opposed racist discrimination.[9]

In response to these protests, the Summers' landlady decided against eviction. A member of the St. Catharines Armenian community, she and her family acknowledged that she had acted hastily. The anonymous racist letters frightened her precisely because her own community had suffered from discrimination.

The deputation that John Ideson led to City Hall on 26 October 1959 enjoyed the support of the St. Catharines and District Labour Council, the local Ministerial Association, the United Nations Association of St. Catharines, the Unitarian Fellowship of St. Catharines, the St. Catharines Council of Women, the Niagara District Council of Human Rights, B'nai Brith of St. Catharines (a Jewish organization), and the local Bahais.[10] The deputation called for a by-law that would make it illegal to select tenants for or eject tenants from apartment buildings and multiple dwelling units because of their race, colour, religion, or national origin. The legislation would also authorize municipal officials to investigate reported cases of discrimination and to fine violators. The proposal received strong endorsement from Alderman Joe Reid, who claimed that St. Catharines was not "very far away from Little Rock."[11] Reid was referring to Little Rock, Arkansas, where jeering whites, supported by the state governor, attempted to bar nine African American students from entering the local high school under federal court order.

But the Summers case also revealed that many Canadians still refused to acknowledge that racism was a problem in Canada. Such St. Catharines notables as the mayor and several aldermen condemned racist discrimination and suggested that the anonymous letters were the work of marginal individuals. The mayor added that the attempt to evict the Summers family was a "misunderstanding," since there was no serious discrimination in St. Catharines. Some aldermen voiced strong opposition to the by-law proposed by Ideson's delegation. According to one of them, while such a law would give "a coloured man the right he should have," it would take away property rights from another person. "It is unfortunate," he argued, "but the minute a coloured person moves into a neighbourhood the fellow next door couldn't sell his home for half what it's worth. Why should the law make me do something that would depress the value of my neighbour's property?" Voicing the views of many Canadian critics of anti-discrimination laws, another alderman protested that one cannot legislate against prejudice.[12] As human rights activists and the victims of discrimination pointed out, however, legislation was designed to eliminate discrimination, not prejudice. Although such legislation did have an educational function — to publicize the state's condemnation of discrimination — the victims of racism could not afford to await the slow change of attitudes as a result of education.

In the end, the by-law proposal was defeated by one vote, apparently because the majority of council members believed that such a law was beyond the jurisdiction of municipal government. However, they agreed to support a petition to extend the provincial Fair Accommodation Practices Act, which outlawed the refusal of services in public places on the basis of race, creed, colour, nationality, ancestry or place of origin, to cover apartment rental. When the petition was submitted to Ontario Premier Leslie Frost later that year, St. Catharines organizations, the District Labour Council foremost among them, were disproportionately represented among those who supported it. The proposed change was enacted provincially in 1961.[13]

The Labour Council was much slower to take action against gender discrimination in the workplace. Contrary to the common view of the 1950s as an era of domesticity, in blue-collar communities such as St. Catharines the number of women, including married women, in paid employment grew. Employers needed their work, and many supervisors came to believe that married women were more reliable workers than single ones. Yet, as in earlier decades, the need for their labour did not lead to improved conditions. Assumptions about women's nature and abilities were too deeply rooted among employers and workers.

A statement by Martin Cahill, public relations director of McKinnon Industries, illustrates such assumptions. "Most of the jobs that require nimbleness and fine attention to small detail are done by girls," he told a *Standard* reporter. "Girls don't do laborious or heavy work," he added, explaining that they had done such work during World War II only "because of the man shortage." [14] Evidently, this departure from the norm failed to convince him that women were capable of performing supposedly "male jobs." Such assumptions help to explain why the sex-typing of jobs continued at McKinnon until the 1970s and why women were limited to a small number of jobs in just a few departments.

In October 1967, a group of female workers who lost their jobs at McKinnon Industries used the hearings of the Royal Commission on the Status of Women in Canada to publicize discrimination against women on production lines in the automotive industry. They received assistance in drafting their brief from feminist Laura Sabia, a former St. Catharines municipal councillor.

In May 1966, with no advance notice whatever, we were suddenly laid off. We were not even given the courtesy of 24 hours' notice. Some of us with seniority of 5 to 10 years were also laid off without any explanation save that there was no longer any work for us. We were told to apply as new employees in other cities, but because of family ties, this was impossible for us. We appealed to Local 199 of the United Automobile Workers Union for some explanation and redress. We were told of our eligibility for Unemployment Insurance Benefits and Transitional Assistance Benefits. We were made aware of the government's retraining program in various commercial and stenography courses. The U.A.W. was aware of the impending Auto Pact and its ramification for women workers, but they did little to solve these problems with industry.

We are cognizant of the government's clerical courses for women, but girls coming out of school with a four-year commercial diploma find employment at $40.00 to $50.00 per week, which, we submit, is not adequate for us to maintain a home and support a family. We do not want to be a drain on welfare agencies. We want only to support our families in dignity and we assure you that we are most willing to do the hard work that industry entails. . . .

We submit to you that women in industry are subject to discrimination as far as lay-offs are concerned. The first to go are women, and rarely are they called back. Unions care little of forcing an issue where women are concerned.

We ask that a thorough study be made of women workers on production lines in industry. Industry cares little of making available jobs for women when certain lines are closed off. Women seem expendable in both industry and unions.[15]

The twelve women who signed the brief were all self-supporting, some of them with dependent families. Their representative, Ann Fast, spoke at the commission's hearings in Toronto. She explained that following the signing of the Auto Pact, when the automotive industry was being restructured, women were seriously disadvantaged at McKinnon Industries because the sex-typing of jobs meant that there were two seniority lists. Since so few job classifications were open to women, they were much more likely to lose their jobs than men with equal (or greater) seniority. But while the women demanded an end to such "discrimination between the sexes," they also endorsed the ideal of the family wage by recommending that "married women, supported by a husband, should step aside to allow room for the woman who must support herself and her family."[16] The self-supporting women apparently believed that married women working for "luxuries" were not committed to their jobs. The Royal Commission was unwilling to support the rights of self-supporting women over those of married women, but it suggested that the elimination of gender-based job descriptions and seniority lists would improve the situation at McKinnon Industries.

Ann Fast also told the commission that the UAW showed little interest in women's problems. Such complaints elicited little sympathy from D. F. Hamilton, secretary-treasurer of the Ontario Federation of Labour (OFL), who presented the next brief to the

Royal Commission. Showing little understanding of the demands of the double day on female heads of family, Hamilton unwittingly confirmed Fasts's allegations by suggesting that unions would be more responsive to women's needs if women were "willing to spend their off-hours, as men do, working for the union."

The entry of growing numbers of married women into paid employment in the years that followed finally led to greater recognition of the right of all women, single or married, to equal opportunities in the work force. More women came to hold executive positions in unions, and unions pushed for equal pay for work of equal value, maternity leave, and access to child care.

# Ideologies Clashing:
# The 1970 UAW Strike

The fierce ideological divisions of the Cold War continued to colour the political orientation of organized labour in Niagara well into the 1970s. A 1970 UAW strike is illustrative of this point. UAW Local 199 was, by far, the largest union in Niagara, representing thousands of workers at General Motors (GM, formerly McKinnon Industries) in St. Catharines. In the early 1970s, internal ideological divisions in Local 199 were starker than ever before. Activists were divided into two competing factions: the Unity caucus and the Walter Reuther Administration caucus.[1]

The Unity caucus was made up of communists, socialists, and an assortment of anti-capitalist radicals, some of whom took jobs at GM in order to engage in class struggle at the level of the shop floor. Before the 1970 strike, the Unity caucus was a powerful political force in the plant and regularly bested the Walter Reuther Administration caucus in in-plant elections.

The strength of the Unity caucus was not necessarily attributable to the political and ideological orientation of its leadership but rather to its commitment to an adversarial brand of union-management relations that routinely paid dividends for workers. The Walter Reuther Administration caucus, named after fiercely anti-communist UAW President Walter Reuther, was made up of union activists, mostly social democrats, who rejected the radical anti-capitalist ideology promoted by the leadership of the Unity caucus.[2]

After the sudden death of Walter Reuther in May 1970, his successor, Leonard Woodcock, led UAW members in a historic strike against GM. The autoworkers had not struck GM for over two decades, but resentment between the workers and the company had been simmering beneath the surface for years. Production at GM was stopped on 15 September 1970 when 6,600 UAW Local 199 members in St. Catharines, and 350,000 of their counterparts throughout North America, walked off the job in a legal strike.[3]

In the United States, the strike, which lasted ten weeks, led to an improved contract that included cost-of-living allowances and a pension plan that gave workers the option of retiring after thirty years of service, regardless of their age. When, south of the border, the UAW strike against GM ended on 20 November, the Canadian section of the UAW refused to settle and continued their strike. Gord Lambert, a fiery communist, leader of the local 199 Unity caucus, and chair of the UAW's Master Bargaining Committee in Canada, was the driving force behind the decision to prolong the strike in Canada. Canadian autoworkers were seeking, among other things, wage parity with their American counterparts.[4]

To qualify for strike pay, autoworkers were required to picket two hours per week and to attend union education courses that, according to the St. Catharines Standard, ranged from "trade union history to an explanation of the Canada Pension Plan and highway safety."[5] Single men received $30 per week strike pay; married men received $35; and married men with children received $40 per week.[6] (The local media omitted information about strike pay for women.) The extended strike in Canada came to an end on 16 December 1970. Although local autoworkers endorsed the contract by a vote of 5,101 to 377 a few days later as part of a ratification meeting, the settlement failed to win immediate wage parity with American autoworkers and included a cost-of-living concession.[7]

The prolonged strike in Canada had a profound impact on internal union politics at Local 199. Most local autoworkers viewed it as a failure. Gord Lambert began to lose support in the plant for the way in which bargaining had been handled at the national level. Lambert was a strong rank-and-file leader who served as plant chairman for eighteen years, vice president of Local 199 for eighteen years, head of the UAW's Master Level Bargaining Committee for GM in Canada for eighteen years, and later as president of the St. Catharines and District Labour Council for five years.[8] Immediately after the 1970 strike, Lambert's opponents from the Walter Reuther Administration caucus managed to convince the majority of rank-and-file workers in the plant that Lambert's ideological brand of militancy was outdated and ineffective. Rumours even circulated suggesting that his drive to prolong the strike in Canada had been influenced by the Communist Party.[9]

Lambert was defeated in his bid to be re-elected to the plant chairman position by John Washuta, who later became president of Local 199 and a St. Catharines city councillor. Washuta was a member of the Walter Reuther Administration caucus which was renamed the Blue Slate caucus after the 1970 strike. The Blue Slate caucus gained control of the Bargaining Committee in the 1971 elections and of the local's executive in 1972; both had previously been dominated by the more radical Unity slate.[10]

The events of the early 1970s had a paralyzing effect on the Unity caucus. Internal dissent and growing ideological schisms marginalized the left and led to its eventual decline over the course of the next two decades. By the 1990s, the slate system for Local 199 elections had all but disappeared, with candidates preferring to run as independents.[11] Local 199 had been one of the last bastions of left politics within the autoworkers union; it never managed to recover from the fallout over the 1970 strike. Most Unity caucus activists eventually drifted to the St. Catharines and District Labour Council, where they proved to be a far more formidable force throughout the 1970s, organizing a local boycott of California grapes to help raise the wages of farm workers, building international solidarity with anti-colonial struggles around the world, aggressively pursuing an anti-racism agenda, and forming a union of the unemployed.[12]

The ideological shift that took place within Local 199 in the 1970s had been well underway in the rest of the labour movement, as evidenced by organized labour's postwar effort to rid unions of communist leadership and its growing support for social democracy as the dominant political orientation of the Canadian labour movement. While radical forces within the autoworkers union unquestionably lost control over the ideological direction of Local 199, they continued to play an integral role in building union power on the shop floor, organizing and mobilizing rank-and-file support for political action campaigns and future strike actions.

## Strike Wave: 1972–76

The right to strike, although controversial, is unquestionably the most powerful form of leverage available to union members given the power imbalance inherent in the employment relationship. As we have seen, work stoppages triggered by strikes are designed to disrupt business production or the provision of services in an effort to exert pressure on an employer to come to an agreement with the union on the terms and conditions of work. Strike action, which in the postwar period became regulated by a strict legal framework, normally takes place in response to a critical impasse in collective bargaining and is best understood as a last, but often necessary, resort when a union and an employer cannot reach a negotiated agreement.

Between 1972 and 1976, a total of 4,751 strikes and lockouts, each involving, on average, eight hundred workers, were launched in Canada.[1] In Niagara, workers at Court Industries Limited, members of Local 268 of the International Association of Machinists and Aerospace Workers (IAM), walked picket lines in 1972 along with Local 582 of the International Chemical Workers, who were engaged in a dispute with their employer, Exolon. Labour disputes also took place at Seaway News, Red-D-Mix Concrete, and Kimberly-Clark of Canada over the course of the year. In 1973, UAW Local 199 struck Aimco Industries, and the USWA struck Foster Wheeler.[2] In the same year, moving picture operators, members of International Alliance of Theatrical Stage Employees (IATSE), walked picket lines to settle a contract dispute with local theatres, and a Canada-wide railroad strike had a profound impact on St. Catharines. In 1974, workers at GM, Columbus McKinnon Limited, Hayes Dana, Aimco Industries, Kelsey-Hayes, Eaton Yale, W. S. Tyler Company, Foster Wheeler, and several credit unions walked picket lines. The next year, painters and allied workers, postal workers, sheet metal workers, paperworkers, autoworkers, and plumbers were all engaged in labour disputes with a variety of employers across the Niagara Region.[3] Strikes continued in the paper industry in 1976 at Abitibi Provincial Paper, Domtar Pulp and Paper, Beaver Wood Fibre, and the Ontario Paper Company. Steelworkers at Ferranti Packard walked picket lines along with members of Local 1263 of the Canadian Union of Public Employees (CUPE) working for the Regional Municipality of Niagara. In short, between 1972 and 1976, thousands of workers across Niagara were involved in prolonged and bitter labour disputes with their employers.

This strike wave in Niagara, and indeed across Canada, had immediately preceded a recession in the early 1970s that saw unemployment increase substantially along with inflation. Workers looked to the collective bargaining process to ensure that they could maintain a decent standard of living amid economic crises, but their employers were equally determined to make certain their profit margins remained high.

The strike wave also coincided with a shift in the way the state handled labour relations. A key aspect of repressive government policy was back-to-work legislation, an ad hoc law that forces an end to a labour dispute. Back-to-work legislation was used much more frequently by federal and provincial governments during this period. In fact, during the 1970s, federal and provincial governments ended a large number of labour disputes by handing down no less than forty-one back-to-work measures. This compared to thirteen back-to-work measures passed in the 1960s and just three in the 1950s.[4] On 14 October 1975, much to the delight of Canada's business elite, Pierre Trudeau's Liberal government announced the introduction of a program of wage-and-price controls in an effort to curb inflation. Prime Minister Trudeau's Anti-Inflation Program, which suspended free collective bargaining for workers, signaled the introduction of neoliberalism to Canada. A new right-wing, anti-union, political and economic ideology, neoliberalism, strongly promoted in the United States by President Ronald Reagan and in Britain by Prime Minister Margaret Thatcher, favoured the weakening and gradual elimination of the social safety net, as well as a reorientation of government policy to meet the needs of corporations. Privatization, deregulation, and free trade all represent important policy pillars in the neoliberal playbook.

In many ways, Trudeau embraced neoliberalism through his anti-labour policies such as the "6 and 5" program, so called because it limited wage increases for civil servants to 6 percent in the first year and 5 percent in the second, despite high levels of inflation in the early 1980s. The federal government also temporarily removed the right to strike for public sector workers and passed a number of other pieces of legislation that restricted union rights.[5]

Canada's provinces took their cue from the federal government and quickly implemented their own coercive policies aimed at organized labour. These actions included the virtual removal of the right to strike in some sectors and continued wage restraint.

Governments of all political stripes used words like "voluntarism" to hide their real agenda of coercion. This shift in government policy also resulted in a fundamental reversal of roles. In the postwar era, the demands of labour unions were appeased in order to maintain capitalism as a viable economic system. The new ideology shifted the focus by forcing unions to take responsibility for maintaining capitalism.[6]

Many workers resisted this economic and political shift by engaging in mass strikes and mobilizations against employers and governments. For example, on 13 May 1974, workers at Abitibi Provincial Paper in Thorold engaged in a controversial wildcat strike that shut down the plant for four days. Six hundred workers walked off the job after four of their co-workers were suspended for refusing to carry out additional duties assigned by management.[7] The incident involving the workers, who defied back-to-work orders issued by their local executive and their national representative, foreshadowed a year of labour unrest in Ontario's pulp and paper industry. A month earlier, in April 1974, Canadian pulp and paper workers, with the help of a Thorold-based union representative named Don Holder, broke away from the United Paperworkers International Union to form the Canadian Paperworkers Union (CPU). The fractious birth of the CPU, which came about through a desire for more autonomy, was an exciting development for union activists, but the new union would not have the luxury of celebrating its birth for very long. With virtually no strike funds available to help support its members, owing to an asset dispute with the international union, the CPU would take on the pulp and paper industry in an unprecedented labour struggle that would drag on for nearly eight months.[8]

On 14 October 1976, the first anniversary of the Trudeau government's announcement that it would implement a program of wage-and-price controls, the Canadian labour movement held a day of protest that drew tens of thousands of workers off the job across the country. The Canadian Labour Congress (CLC), Canada's largest central labour organization, claimed that more than one million workers took part in industrial actions, including an estimated 400,000 workers in Ontario.[9] Some Niagara workers traveled to Ottawa to join thousands of other workers demonstrating on Parliament Hill. Others engaged in a series of workplace actions in Niagara.

In an impressive display of union power, autoworkers led the way by shutting down production at GM, Hayes Dana, and a number of other manufacturing plants in the Niagara region. The *St. Catharines Standard* reported that only 190 of 3,500 day-shift workers at GM bothered to show up for work.[10] Steelworkers managed to disrupt production at Niagara Structural Steel, Lord and Burnham, and Seneca Steel, in Beamsville. Bus drivers, caretakers, and maintenance workers who failed to report to work created disruptions for the four local school boards.[11] The strike wave across Niagara and the rest of Canada was complemented by organizing initiatives and direct actions against rogue employers.

In 1972, in an apparent effort to avoid unionization of its part-time secretarial staff, the Welland County Roman Catholic Separate School Board fired its forty-three part-time secretaries only to rehire them all from a temporary agency.[12] In protest, Niagara area labour councils presented the board with a brief threatening a tax transfer drive.[13] That is, area unions would encourage their members to switch their taxes from the separate school board to the public board. Although the separate school board went ahead with its plan to fire its secretaries, CUPE, the union seeking to represent the workers, brought the case to the Ontario Labour Relations Board (OLRB). The board ruled that, notwithstanding the peculiar outsourcing ploy used by the separate school board, the workers were indeed employees of the board. Part-time secretarial staff became the newest members of CUPE shortly thereafter.

In November 1972, the manager of the Skyway Lumber Company became a target of the St. Catharines and District Labour Council when he refused to allow fifteen workers time off to vote in the federal election on 30 October. One of the workers complained to the area returning officer that he was forced to quit his job in order to exercise his democratic right to vote. Labour Council President Kenneth Brisbois wrote to the manager of Skyway Lumber on 2 November 1972, stating that the council "has a policy of protecting not only the organized but also the unorganized against arrogant and unscrupulous employers." [14] He added that "this Council will not tolerate any employer violating [the Elections] Act, or any legislation that is enacted for the benefit of all the people in this country." Brisbois called on the manager to write a letter of apology and pay each worker for two extra hours or risk legal action. The manager, who had initially complained to the *St. Catharines Standard* that he could not afford to close his business to comply with the law, responded to the Labour Council's request almost immediately. On 6 November, the manager wrote to the Labour Council and enclosed fifteen letters of apology with a promise to pay each worker for an additional two hours on their next pay cheque.[15]

During this period, the Labour Council also made a habit of helping out non-union hospitality workers involved in individual disputes with their employers. The Labour Council routinely wrote letters of warning to employers who engaged in unfair labour practices and helped workers file Employment Standards appeals. This type of activity cultivated a "fight back" culture within the local labour movement and solidified organized labour's place as a political force within the community.

# Canadian Pulp and Paper
# Workers Fight Back

By the mid-1970s, inflation had been eating away at wage increases in the pulp and paper industry to such a degree that workers had lost roughly $1.75 per hour since 1973.[1] When the workers asked their employers to address the decline in real wages, the giant paper companies refused to budge and, in some instances, hid behind the federal government's Anti-Inflation Board, arguing that they were prohibited from meeting workers' demands.[2]

In Thorold, seven hundred members of CPU Local 290 at Abitibi Provincial Paper legally struck their employer on 17 July 1975. In late August, Abitibi suspended premium payments for striking employees' life insurance.[3] During a campaign stop, Ontario NDP leader Stephen Lewis, flanked by local candidate Mel Swart, addressed the striking workers and accused Abitibi of bargaining in bad faith. Lewis declared that Abitibi "is deliberately and methodically attempting to destroy a new Canadian union and no government worth its salt should permit it."[4]

Workers went for six weeks without any strike pay. To make up for the shortage of strike funds, the 55,000 members of the newly minted union voluntarily donated a minimum of one hour's pay each week to the striking workers in Thorold. The St. Catharines and District Labour Council pledged both moral and financial support. Gord Lambert, the Labour Council's president, told the media, "If Abitibi thinks they can starve the strikers into submission then they . . . are only indulging in wishful thinking."[5]

By mid-September, five thousand CPU members in Ontario were on strike. The dispute that had started in Thorold had spread industry-wide. CPU members at Kimberly-Clark of Canada, Domtar, and Beaver Wood Fibre, all located in Thorold, were walking picket lines along with workers in several northern Ontario communities. Pulp and paperworkers in Québec also hit the picket lines. In all, the labour dispute directly affected two thousand paperworkers in Niagara and indirectly crippled the economy of Thorold, where small businesses were largely dependent on the wages of CPU members.

The Holy Rosary Credit Union extended $500 a month loan credit to striking CPU members, and residents delivered food to the picket line on a daily basis.[6] The community's support for the workers in the labour dispute between the paper mills and the CPU helped deliver a decisive victory to NDP candidate Mel Swart in the

18 September 1975 provincial election. Swart, a vocal supporter of the CPU and a fixture in local politics in Thorold, had run under the CCF-NDP banner in federal and provincial elections on eight separate occasions before finally topping the polls in 1975. His breakthrough represented the NDP's first electoral victory in Niagara.

At the 1 October 1975 meeting of the St. Catharines and District Labour Council, a representative from CPU Local 290 updated delegates on the labour dispute and thanked UAW Local 199 "for its excellent financial and moral support at the plant gate collections."[7] More than $5,000 was raised for the paperworkers. As the strike lengthened, Local 199 offered to advertise odd jobs for CPU members in the union newsletter. In December 1975, the Labour Council made a $1,000 contribution to the strikers, and one of its affiliates announced that it would be donating one hundred Christmas turkeys.[8] A second round of plant gate collections followed.

In February 1976, the industry-wide pulp and paper strike finally came to an end when 3,800 members of thirteen CPU locals in Ontario and Québec cast their ballots 83 percent in favour of ending the labour dispute. In the end, the workers won a modest wage increase and an indexing formula to prevent skyrocketing inflation from reducing wages.

# Corporate Restructuring and Labour's Decline

While Niagara's labour movement was able to demonstrate a degree of social, economic, and political power in the community throughout the 1970s, toward the end of the decade anti-union employers and their allies in government set out to reverse organized labour's gains in an unprecedented way. A combination of high unemployment and the rise of neoliberalism created an increasingly hostile climate for unions. The greatest test of labour's strength came during deep recessionary periods in the early 1980s and early 1990s.

In 1980, GM initiated a major layoff that had a significant impact on the Niagara region. With unemployment hovering just under 20 percent in the St. Catharines-Niagara area in 1981, the St. Catharines and District Labour Council asked government to fund work projects in order to assist laid-off workers in obtaining the number of weeks of employment needed to requalify for unemployment insurance benefits, which were set to expire at the end of January 1982.[1] Around the same time, several autoworkers from St. Catharines joined a "marathon of despair" to protest high interest rates, which were crippling homeowners and precipitating plant closures and layoffs. St. Catharines and District Labour Council President Len Harrison, who helped organize the marathon of runners who took turns jogging from St. Catharines to the Scarborough home of Minister of Housing Paul Cosgrove, dropped off a telegram to the minister demanding his resignation.[2] The prime minister later removed Cosgrove from responsibility for the Canada Housing and Mortgage Corporation and ultimately, in 1983, shuffled him out of the cabinet altogether.

The cabinet shuffle did little to help autoworkers in Niagara, who took another hit with GM's announcement that it was planning to close its Welland Avenue plant in St. Catharines. In June 1982, an estimated twelve hundred UAW members and supporters participated in a march from the UAW hall on Bunting Road in St. Catharines to the Welland Avenue plant.[3] Protesting autoworkers continued to blame the Trudeau government's failure to address high interest rates for the plant closing. Many union members waved placards that read, "Export Trudeau, not our jobs!"[4]

By December 1982, the unemployment rate in St. Catharines-Niagara had risen to just over 20 percent. According to Statistics Canada, the Niagara region ranked second of thirty-two areas across Canada in terms of unemployment.[5] The consistently high levels of joblessness prompted the St. Catharines and District Labour Council to organize a union of the unemployed in order to pressure government to initiate a number of anti-poverty measures, which included extending unemployment insurance benefits, eliminating regressive sales taxes on Canadian-made products, and lowering interest rates. Nearly one hundred unemployed workers packed the UAW hall for the inaugural meeting of the new group. Within the next few months, the Labour Council managed to launch the Unemployed Help Centre with the assistance of progressive church organizations and government.[6] The drop-in centre for unemployed workers provided job listings, counselling, and a soup kitchen.

St. Catharines workers protesting Trudeau's economic policies, June 1982. Courtesy of the St. Catharines Museum (*St. Catharines Standard* Collection).

Although the economic recession was over by the mid-1980s, the election of Brian Mulroney's Conservative government in 1984 signaled that the war against working families was not about to abate. The Mulroney government led an unprecedented attack on Canada's social safety net and embarked on the most ambitious privatization spree in Canadian history.[7] In 1987, the government negotiated a free trade agreement with the United States. Serving to benefit corporate interests in both Canada and the United States, the negotiation of a free trade deal guaranteed corporate Canada unrestricted access to the American economy while also providing corporate interests in the United States greater access to Canada's vast resources. The Canadian labour movement joined progressive community groups and political organizations to fight the free trade deal, proposing instead that Canada achieve a "fair trade" deal that would protect Canadian sovereignty and Canadian workers.[8] The labour movement in Niagara organized vigorously against the free trade agreement, holding a number of town hall meetings to raise awareness about the impact of free trade on the local economy. NDP candidates won a record high share of the popular vote in the 1988 federal election, which was considered a referendum on free trade. However, the anti–free trade forces split between the NDP and the Liberals, thus allowing the Conservatives to form a second majority government despite winning only 43 percent of the popular vote. The labour movement's all-out war against the Canada-US free trade agreement in the late 1980s, although ultimately unsuccessful, demonstrated the labour movement's strength as an independent, progressive coalition builder. As for the trade deal, it precipitated massive layoffs in Ontario's manufacturing sector, while failing to liberalize trade in key areas, such as softwood lumber. Union membership in Niagara dropped dramatically as a result of the trade deal, as the manufacturing sector began to shrink at an alarming rate. In the face of deindustrialization, unions increasingly looked toward the growing service sector as an area of potential growth.

# The Eaton's Strike:

# Women Workers Walk the Line

In 1984, the Retail, Wholesale and Department Store Union (RWDSU) actively began organizing retail service workers at Eaton's locations across Ontario. The growing service sector, dominated by women and part-time workers, was seen as the labour movement's greatest organizing challenge in the postwar period, largely because of the high level of turnover and relatively small number of employees working at individual locations. Despite these obstacles, the RWDSU helped workers at six Eaton's locations, including one store in St. Catharines, to win union certification in the spring of 1984. Workers were generally upset at the working conditions in Eaton's stores but were particularly motivated by their employers' unwillingness to provide job security or pensions.

Eaton's refused to negotiate a master agreement with the union, which would have covered all Eaton's workers at every unionized outlet, preferring instead to negotiate separate contracts at each unionized store. This decentralized approach favoured the employer because it divided workers by location. However, the union was able to unite the predominantly female workforce around common issues, and union members agreed to a coordinated bargaining strategy that would force Eaton's to bargain with them as a group. Unionized Eaton's workers at six locations in Brampton, Toronto, London, and St. Catharines walked off the job on 30 November 1984. The plan was to disrupt normal business operations at the six stores and picket unorganized stores.

At a 4 January 1985 rally outside the Eaton's store at the Pen Centre in St. Catharines, CLC official Shirley Carr declared, "I hope Fred Eaton choked on his Christmas or New Year's turkey."[1] The demonstrators then moved from the picket lines into the mall to take their message directly to shoppers. Labour activists and community groups returned in February 1985 to bolster picket lines

Picketers from Niagara-area unions demonstrate their displeasure
with Eaton's at the Pen Centre in St. Catharines.
Courtesy of the St. Catharines and District Labour Council.

and once again bring their case to consumers. This time, however, Eaton's was ready with beefed-up security and police. Chanting, "Hey, hey, ho, ho, Eaton's scabs have got to go," demonstrators made their way past security and through the halls of the Pen Centre.[2] The Niagara Regional Police waited until after the demonstration to charge Canadian Auto Workers (CAW) Local 199 President Gerry Michaud and an RWDSU organizer with trespassing.[3] Despite the militant actions of the labour movement, Eaton's workers continued to enjoy strong support from the community. Welland-Thorold NDP MPP Mel Swart endorsed the strike, likening the labour dispute to a battle between David and Goliath.[4]

On 12 March 1985, a group of women workers from the St. Catharines Eaton's store began a protest walk to Toronto, dubbed a "trek for fairness." Draped in several layers of clothing and fitted with running shoes, Shelley Adams, one of the striking workers, told the *St. Catharines Standard*, "We've been out now for four months. We want a pension and some job security. It's been a tight battle."[5] The half-dozen women participating in the trek for fairness arrived in Toronto three days later, where they joined a rally at Queen's Park calling for the government to pass first contract legislation. Under such law, a neutral third party would be granted the right to impose a first contract when a union and an employer could not reach an agreement. Such legislation is intended to guard newly unionized (and often vulnerable) workers against union-busting. However, the union recognized that it could not rely exclusively on the law to win its struggle against Eaton's.

On 13 April 1985, Niagara's four labour councils organized yet another rally in support of striking Eaton's workers in St. Catharines. The rally, which drew more than three hundred people, boosted morale on the picket line, where workers had been faithfully holding the fort for twenty weeks.[6]

The "Eaton's Fairness Campaign" became an issue during the 1985 provincial election, and union activists took the opportunity to raise awareness about the strike and its impact on the company's primarily female, part-time workers. Strikers also took the opportunity to press politicians on their support for first contract legislation. The RWDSU distributed hundreds of "Boycott Eaton's" lawn signs and ran radio advertisements encouraging shoppers in Niagara to steer clear of Eaton's.[7] The Eaton's strike was about lifting women workers out of the low-wage, casual service and retail sector. Unionization was seen as a way of achieving decent pensions and job security for workers in a traditionally unorganized industry. Although the union succeeded in winning support from the community, Eaton's relentless and hard-nosed approach to bargaining with its newly unionized employees convinced the union's leadership to give up the fight.

In May 1985, the labour dispute came abruptly to an end when the president of the international RWDSU signed a contract that was basically the same as the one Eaton's had offered the union in November 1984.[8] Rather than ask union members to ratify the agreement, the union instead asked its members to vote on whether they wished to return to work. Under Ontario labour law, Eaton's could decide not to rehire striking workers if their labour dispute exceeded six months. With that deadline fast approaching, workers opted overwhelmingly to return to work in order to save their jobs.

The Eaton's strike and similar organizing drives in banks were significant because they highlighted the labour movement's new focus on organizing women workers. That focus was reinforced in 1986, when Shirley Carr, a CUPE activist and Niagara Falls native, succeeded Dennis McDermott as president of the CLC. Carr, who had played a central role in organizing employees of the Regional Municipality of Niagara, was the first woman and the first public sector union member to lead the CLC. Carr served two terms as CLC president before stepping down in 1992.

In 1993, the first contract legislation that Eaton's workers had been lobbying for finally became law under the Ontario NDP government. But it was quickly rescinded once the Mike Harris Conservatives swept to power in 1995.

# "Don't Lower the Standard":
# The Newsroom on Strike

When media tycoon Conrad Black's Hollinger Inc. bought a majority stake in the Southam newspaper chain in November 1996, journalists took notice. By the end of 1996, Black owned 650 dailies and weeklies around the world.[1] He controlled almost half of Canada's daily circulation and 70 percent of Ontario's newspapers, including the *St. Catharines Standard,* which had been locally owned and operated for over a century by the prominent Burgoyne family before being sold in 1996. The change in ownership unshered in dramatic changes for the newspaper's workforce.

Black had a reputation as a ruthless employer who routinely intervened in editorial policy decisions and engaged in severe cost-cutting at the expense of journalists, for whom he had little regard. More and more, journalists saw unionization as a way of protecting both their trade and their jobs in an increasingly hostile work environment.

In 1997, the Communications, Energy and Paperworkers union (CEP), under the guise of the Southern Ontario Newspaper Guild, organized workers in the *St. Catharines Standard* newsroom. A year later, when the *Standard* insisted on wage rate rollbacks, the union had no choice but to strike. The newsroom staff began walking picket lines in May 1998, and stickers reading "Don't Lower the *Standard*" started to appear all over the city. The striking workers picketed a Southam newspaper shareholders' meeting in Toronto, where record profits were reported, while the *Standard* imported scab labour to produce its paper.[2] In an effort to raise awareness of the dispute and put pressure on the *Standard* to settle the contract, the striking workers launched a newspaper of their own, *The Independent*. Striker Andrew Lundy later recounted the experience in a blog post:

In May 1998, the 30-odd newsroom staff at *The Standard* in St. Catharines went on strike — the first time in the paper's 100-plus year history — after talks to come up with a first contract broke down.

The reporters, editors and photographers decided that, in addition to picketing, we'd also start our own strike paper, *The Independent*. There were two main reasons: one, to show the quality of work we were capable of, and two, to drain advertising dollars away from the parent company, hurting them enough to get them bargaining from a more acceptable position.

Working on the paper was one of the hardest things I ever did. While also a member of the bargaining committee, I routinely pulled 18-hour days (as did many of my colleagues) reporting, editing and laying out the paper. Most of the striking reporters wrote good stories, the copy desk edited and laid out a quality publication, and the photogs produced some great pics. We even had an advertising guy who recently retired from *The Standard* helping sell our ad space.

We published three weekly issues, each of which broke news that *The Standard* (then staffed by replacement workers and managers) did not, and featured several local advertisers who diverted their money away from *The Standard*.

The paper was distributed free, so we couldn't rightly claim to be cutting into the main newspaper, but the ads did help pay for our costs, along with the generous help of CEP (Communications, Energy and Paperworkers), our union. Once the strike was settled, the paper disappeared.

Overall, it was a fun, exhausting, and most would say worthwhile experience.[3]

*The Independent* was launched on 30 May 1998. Paul O'Brien, Unit Chair of CEP Local 87-M, explained in the first edition of the newspaper that the idea for producing *The Independent* came from striking newsroom workers in Welland, who had created the *Guardian Express* years earlier in order to exert pressure on their employer to settle a contract.[4] The now-defunct *Guardian Express* was so well received by the community that it continued to operate for nearly a decade after the strike. In the case of *The Independent,* the union published roughly 45,000 copies of the twenty-page tabloid-style newspaper, which were distributed weekly, free of charge. The newspaper talked about the labour dispute but also tackled community-wide issues such as restructuring in the automotive sector, cruelty to animals, and mould in portable classrooms.

According to an article in the first edition of *The Independent,* "the main issues of the labour dispute included wage rollbacks of up to 12 percent for new employees, threats to the photography department, and a gag order that journalists fear attacks the very basis of their craft — free speech."[5] Unions, community groups, and small businesses kept the weekly newspaper afloat through advertising. In one advertisement, the Niagara New Democratic Youth injected some humour into the politically charged strike by asking: "Q: What's the difference between Conrad Black and a trampoline? A: You should always take your shoes off before jumping on a trampoline."[6]

After a three-week strike, the *Standard* reached a deal with its newsroom staff, and the union ceased publication of the *Independent* shortly after its 13 June 1998 edition was distributed to the community. Even though most of the workers were proud of their first contract, which included improvements to benefits and language in the collective agreement, roughly a third of them took buyouts or simply left shortly after the strike. Although the union was forced to accept a two-tiered wage system in order to settle the contract, the disparity between the tiers that management was proposing was narrowed significantly as a result of the strike. More importantly, the union remained intact. A strike involving the same publisher, which took place at the *Calgary Herald* shortly after the *Standard* strike, ended with the newspaper breaking the back of the union. The newsroom workers at the *Standard* not only avoided decertification but actually improved their union contract in several key areas.

# Occupation in Thorold

Down the road in Thorold, CEP members working at the Gallaher Thorold Paper Company (formerly Abitibi Provincial Paper) were bracing for a bombshell announcement from the plant ownership. On 25 May 1999, Gallaher Paper declared bankruptcy and shut down operations. Three hundred members of CEP Local 290 would be left jobless, but the workers were not prepared to go down without a fight.

Bankruptcy trustee Ernst and Young and creditor Toronto Dominion Bank became targets of the workers' anger when Niagara Centre NDP MPP Peter Kormos suggested that the creditor was favouring bids by companies that wanted to liquidate the plant rather than run it.[1] In the early morning of Monday, 18 October, a group of union members occupied the plant. The workers moved quickly to secure the plant by locking all gates and doors with chains. Heavy machinery was strategically placed in front of bay doors, but not before a large supply of coffee, clothing, and communications equipment made its way into the mill. CEP representative Mike Lambert told the media that the workers would stay until "smoke is once again coming from the stacks."[2] The workers used masking tape to spell the words "SAVE JOBS" in an office window and hung a large banner from the mill that read, "Toronto Dominion Bank $1.48 billion profit. What About Us?"[3]

The plant occupation became an overnight media sensation, with the workers being featured on the front cover of the *Globe and Mail*.[4] By shedding light on the impact of the manufacturing crisis on workers' lives, CEP members inspired labour activists across the country to hold companies accountable to the communities in which they operate. Members of Local 290 addressed town hall meetings and picketed TD Bank locations to gain support and educate the public. They even kept the machinery working, conscious of the fact that if it were left dormant, the new owner would be required to spend millions of dollars to get it working again.[5] Meanwhile, the community of Thorold rallied to support their neighbours, locked inside the mill, by delivering cooked meals and other essential supplies. In response to the overwhelming support showed by the community, the workers unfurled yet another banner: "Your total support has been a hit. CEP Local 290 will never forget."[6]

Members of CEP Local 290 occupy the Gallaher Thorold Paper Company in October 1999. Courtesy of Denis Cahill, *St. Catharines Standard.*

Twenty-six days after the occupation began, the workers emerged from the plant after a purchase agreement was finalized. On 11 November 1999, a letter of intent to buy Gallaher was signed by The Butler Group, which signalled its intention to restart the mill. By the following spring, the deal had fallen through.

Cec Makowski, an Ontario vice president of CEP, looked back at the occupation and considered its importance for the labour movement. "When all other avenues have been closed there are still opportunities to achieve a successful outcome by taking a different approach, even if it's illegal. People often say, 'Hey, that's illegal.' I often say, 'Yeah, it's illegal. But your forefathers did a lot of illegal things for the labour movement. In fact, unions themselves were illegal at one time." [7]

On the surface, most of the key labour struggles of the 1970s, 1980s, and 1990s discussed in this book could be characterized as defeats for the unions and the workers involved. Autoworkers held out for several extra weeks in 1970 and gained very little in return; workers at Eaton's walked picket lines for over five months without winning any substantial contract gains; a handful of striking journalists opted to leave their jobs rather than live under a new contract; and the occupation of the Gallaher paper mill did not ultimately result in a new buyer. These examples may even provide fodder for those who contend that unions have outlived their usefulness. However, to treat these labour disputes as outright labour defeats would be to ignore the deep impact that these struggles had both inside and outside of the workplace. Fighting back does make a difference. If unions consistently succumbed to the inevitability of the corporate agenda, workers would eventually give in to the lie that they have no control over their working lives or the political and economic imperatives that inform them. The reality is that workers who stand strong and take part in pivotal labour disputes almost always help prevent further attacks on unions in other workplaces. And not fighting back at all could leave workers worse off than they were before. Labour struggles can also have a profound impact on public opinion and, as the Eaton's strike showed, result in public policy changes. The success of a strike must therefore be measured by what the union gained in the longer term, rather than what it sacrificed in the shorter term.

# Labour Builds Brock:
# Unions and the University

While strikes, lockouts, and picket line confrontations undoubtedly garner the largest labour headlines, the labour movement's
role in giving back to the community, through its commitment to
social unionism, represents an underreported, yet equally important, dimension of union activity. The key role played by Niagara's
labour movement in the establishment of Brock University well
illustrates this point.

In the early 1960s, community leaders in Niagara floated the
idea of building a university that would serve the peninsula. Early
on, the committee responsible for raising funds for the project
identified organized labour as an important source of support.
At the time, there were roughly 40,000 unionized workers in
Niagara, earning an average weekly wage of $95. These workers,
who belonged to 175 locals of fifty-two national and international
unions, were considered essential to a successful fundraising campaign.[1]

Workers were understandably attracted by the prospect of job
creation, but they were also aware that a local university would
make post-secondary education more affordable and keep families
closer together, while at the same time opening doors to higher
education for more of their children. As a fundraising analysis conducted by Brakeley G. A. and Company pointed out, "Many girls
whose families might otherwise be able to educate only their sons
will have the opportunity to attend Brock."[2] Such an argument
was particularly appealing to trade unionists with a traditionally
strong sense of social justice.

In a bid to solidify support from organized labour, Lynn Williams, a staff representative for the USWA, was named organized
labour's representative on the Brock University Founders Committee. The committee believed that financial support in the form of

payroll deductions and in-plant solicitations was the best approach to fundraising among union members. It was estimated that, given a participation rate of 30 percent, unionized workers could be counted on to contribute between $400,000 and $700,000 to the project.[3] However, local unions raised expectations on 22 January 1965, when roughly 125 union activists were invited to a dinner hosted by the Founders Committee. The union activists toured the newly opened Glenridge campus before voting unanimously to support the university's Founding Fund. Local unions agreed to recommend to their respective memberships that each member donate a day's pay to the project each year for the next five years. Organized labour had set a goal of $1,000,000 for itself, far exceeding earlier estimates.[4]

University official Edward Mitchelson explained labour's contribution in an article that appeared in the 1968 edition of the St. Catharines and District Labour Council's *Labour Review*.

Back in the days when the Niagara Peninsula Joint Committee on Higher Education was the only visible sign of the coming of a university, Labour gave its wholehearted endorsement of the founding of Brock. Since then, Labour support in the development and life of the University has continued undiminished. . . .

During the campaign to raise the Founding Fund for Brock, Lynn Williams gave his utmost in leadership. He was assisted by John Ideson of UAW, St. Catharines; Ron Seebach, Steelworkers, Fort Erie; Wilfred "Hap" Hague, Carpenters, Niagara Falls; Fred Butler, Steelworkers, Port Colborne; Arthur Riseley, Public Employees, St. Catharines; Michael Bosnich, UEW, Welland; Howard M. Ashenden, Atlas Steels, Welland, and other leaders and thousands of workers throughout the Peninsula. The success of the Founding Fund bears witness to the interest and dedication of the community-minded people who built the idea of Brock into the real University.[5]

As Williams later recalled, convincing workers to contribute to the establishment of Brock University was easy. "Why wouldn't we do it?" he asked. "This would be a great thing to do for the children of working-class families in the Peninsula. It would allow them to stay in Niagara."[6]

McKinnon workers' contributions to the Brock University Building Fund.
Courtesy of the Brock University Library, Special Collections and Archives.

By 1970, organized labour had surpassed its target, raising $1,410,500 for the university's Founding Fund. This amount represented 21.7 percent of the total amount raised by the Founders Committee. Workers at McKinnon Industries, members of UAW Local 199, led the way with a donation of $518,000.[7] At the time, this amount represented the largest contribution by workers in any single industry to any university in Canada. In return for its generous support, organized labour was given a voice in how the university would be run, in the form of a seat on the university's Board of Trustees.

Labour's seat on the Board of Trustees was originally filled by Lynn Williams, who had himself had the benefit of a university education. After completing undergraduate studies at McMaster University, in Hamilton, Williams went on to pursue graduate studies at the University of Toronto in economics and industrial relations. Before completing his degree, he accepted an assembly line job at the John Inglis plant in Toronto, where he joined Local 2900 of the USWA. Williams went on to work for the CLC and eventually joined the staff of the USWA. It was while he was servicing USWA locals in Niagara in the 1960s that Williams became organized labour's representative on the Founders Committee of Brock University. During his time on the committee, Williams was instrumental in successfully encouraging workers in the Niagara region to contribute, through payroll deductions, to Brock University's Founding Fund. As a member of Brock's first Board of Governors, Williams initiated the Brock Invitational Lectures.[8] He left Niagara in 1973, after being elected district director of the USWA. In 1977, he became international secretary of the union and, in 1984, was elected president of the international union. He was re-elected twice to that position before retiring in 1994. The first Canadian to occupy the USWA's top spot, Williams was awarded an honorary degree from Brock in 1985.

The final report of the Brock University Founding Fund contained the following passage assessing the contribution of Niagara's labour movement to the development of the university:

With the endorsement of Trades and Labour Councils, and a majority of the individual union locals throughout the Peninsula, the Founding Fund had the full support of organized labour. Of equal importance was the willingness of management in most major industries to permit not only an on-the-job canvass of employees, but to arrange for payroll deduction of contributions over a five-year period. In almost every instance where management undertook a strong supporting stand, while encouraging the participation of labour in the plant campaign, success was achieved. Exceptions to this rule developed where plants were undergoing labour difficulties and where relations between management and labour were strained. The only areas where Industrial Employees failed to well exceed were ones in which management refused permission for a thorough in-plant canvass and payroll deduction.

The overall quota of $1,000,000 was well over-subscribed, largely as a result of the splendid example set by the employees of McKinnon Industries Ltd., and the general acceptance of labour of the formula of one day's pay per year for five years as a reasonable gift for each employee.

The Headquarters staff activities of John Ideson, President of the St. Catharines Trades and Labour Council, who served as full-time director of this Division, and the Government and Institutional Employee Division, contributed greatly to the continuing excellent relations with organized labour.[9]

"Managing is too important to leave to the managers," said Williams, who firmly believed that workers ought to have a voice with regard to what goes on in their industries and in their workplaces.[10] In much the same vein, Williams believed that labour's participation in the building of Brock University was integral to ensuring that labour would continue to play an important role in the university's future development. For Williams, education was essential to building a strong labour movement. As he saw it, the university could serve the labour movement by fostering research that would help the local economy to prosper. He also believed that the existence of Brock University would help to diversify Niagara's economy.[11]

In a 6 December 1982 lecture at the University of Toronto, Williams elaborated on his vision for the relationship between universities and the labour movement:

> My ideas about the relationship between the University and the Labour Movement, both in terms of the extent to which there has or has not been a relationship, and of the extent to which there ought to be one, have always revolved around the idea of access.
>
> My view of the university sees it as a wondrously privileged place, the custodian, if you will, of the sum total of the intellectual and cultural accomplishments of our society. Custodians in the nature of things become more than that title may imply — they aren't simply the keepers — they become as well the principal users and interpreters of that for which it is their privilege to be responsible. . . .
>
> . . . My deepest and longest held conviction, with regard to the relationship between the university and the labour movement, is, therefore, that workers and their organizations ought to have equitable access to the storehouse of knowledge and expertise which the university represents, and that, by and large, they do not. . . .
>
> . . . While some progress has been made in terms of the accessibility of working people's children to the university, the sad reality seems to me to be that progress in this direction has been declining in recent years. There are, of course, and unfortunately, a multitude of social and cultural factors involved in this circumstance, and dealing with them is a complex and difficult problem. However, the economic factor of cost is clear and self-evident, and the facts are that, on that basis alone, many people, otherwise qualified and interested, are prevented access.
>
> A few years ago it seemed to me that we were moving well in the direction of providing a much greater equality of opportunity in regard to cost at least. That was the principal reason why those of us active in the labour movement in the Niagara Peninsula at the time of the establishment of Brock University at St. Catharines

encouraged significant labour and community support for that institution. Although I have no statistical evidence one way or the other, I do believe it helped provide more access, as presumably did all the regional universities. . . .

. . . These developments, along with more generous funding by government of loans and scholarships, brought great hope. Regrettably, the days of austerity have produced a number of cutbacks in educational assistance, not the least significant of which have been in the area of student assistance and tuition fees, the result of which must inevitably be to push the university into a more elitist, less open, position. . . .

. . . Limited access has been compounded by limited outreach. If the labour movement and working people have been lacking in access to the university, so too has the university community not reached out to involve itself with working people and the labour movement in any manner equivalent to the level of its involvement with and recognition of other institutions and social groupings. . . .

. . . The gap between the university community and the labour movement, has meant that many in the university have little understanding of what the labour movement is really about. Perceptions of the movement are often very unrealistic, from the classical economists and the business schools on the one hand, who frequently view the trade union as an unnatural and improper interference with the market place, to the radical theorists on the other, who often appear to believe that they have a better appreciation of what the trade union movement is and what it should be about than does the movement itself.

A similar set of attitudes and a similar lack of realistic understanding often apply to working people themselves, as well to their unions. Workers, too, often are seen on one extreme as numbers, for the purposes of the economist or the engineer, or at the other extreme, as romanticized figures in the class struggle.

The reality, of course, is that workers are people, real people, with all the same needs, hopes, dreams and problems that everyone else experiences. . . .

. . . There can be no doubt that the arrival of collective bargaining on the campus is a positive development in terms of the university's awareness of the labour movement, and its long-term relationship with it. Although I recognize that it could not realistically have happened otherwise, I do regret that it is essentially a craft model of collective bargaining which exists on the campus, not an industrial union model.

Jean Gérin-Lajoie, the retired Director of District 5 of our Union which represents our members in Eastern Canada, has recently completed a history of our Union in Quebec. In it he makes the point, which he says emerges clearly from his research, that the industrial union structure, in which all levels of employment are in one organization, requires an examination of the total picture, a concern about the circumstances of all who are involved, in a different way than does the craft approach. His thesis suggests that this is one factor in explaining the traditionally greater concerns of industrial unions, as compared with craft unions, with the broader social and political questions in society. The fact that their bargaining and other union initiatives require them to be concerned with a broad array of problems and issues, not the narrow concerns of one particular group, encourages a more sweeping perspective on other questions as well. A University bargaining group that involved all their employees might be more than a university administration would wish to contemplate, but it surely would require the trade union representatives to develop a knowledgeable understanding of the needs of the total university community.

The view of the university as civilization's storehouse, which I expressed at the beginning of these few remarks, obviously leads to the question, what should the role of the storehouse be?

As I suggested then, it clearly requires those who must care for its contents, and those who must ensure that it receives the additions which are necessary for its currency, and those who must study and reflect upon their meaning. It does not, however, achieve its full purpose if it does not also serve — clearly it does this in the training of its students, and as I have indicated, in its outreach to some elements in the community.

One of my purposes this evening is to suggest that it should continue to improve and expand upon its teaching of labour-related matters to its students and upon its outreach to the labour section of the community.

I am also tempted to suggest, in passing, that the need to reach out more effectively to the labour community might well be viewed as part of the need to reach out in new ways to the problems of society in general, as differentiated from those of particular elites. Is the university, as the resource centre of our accumulated scientific and cultural knowledge, really serving us as well as it should with regard to the critical issues of our time — unemployment, and the horrendous condition of the world economy — the quality of life and the future of our planet — the population explosion and world development — war and peace — in the words of a title of a recent lecture by B. F. Skinner — "Why are we not acting to save the world?"[12]

In 1989, partly in recognition of organized labour's role in building the university, Brock launched the Centre for Labour Studies. Labour education at the post-secondary level had a long tradition in the region, with Niagara College creating the first labour studies program in Canada in 1969.[13] Writing in the St. Catharines and District Labour Council's *Labour Review,* Esther Reiter, a professor of sociology at Brock, provided an intellectual justification for union education at the university level:

As the universities increasingly seek support from the business community in what is called a "partnership," students too often come to view the interests and needs of the business community as one and the same as their own.

There is another side to the story that needs to be told — from the point of view of working people and what their needs and interests are. For example, we have been hearing a great deal about the debt crisis lately, and how we all have to tighten our belts in the new budget. But what does it really mean? Should the burden of our debt be on the shoulders of working people who now face longer waits and lower benefits if they become unemployed? Who benefits when moneys for social welfare programs such as day-care are curtailed?

Trade unionists understand why labour education is so important, and the union movement has been quite effective in educating its members. But an understanding and respect for the struggles of working people is something all can benefit from. University students need to learn about what unions are, what they do, and the rights that trade unions have won for working people. What women can look forward to when they go out into the work world, how the workplace is being restructured — these are some of the issues that need to be critically explored by all students.

Brock University was founded with your help and support. Over 100 union locals in the Niagara region contributed generously to help us get started back in the 1960's. We hope this Labour Studies program will be but one of many bridges between Brock and the Niagara labour community.[14]

Despite organized labour's key role in building Brock University, however, unionization of the university's own workforce came slowly. Maintenance and janitorial staff worked under union contracts early on, but it would be decades before a majority of the university's workforce was unionized.

In 1996, Brock University faculty voted 64 percent in favour of union certification, and the university's professional librarians voted 75 percent in favour of unionization. Brock's faculty and professional librarians chose to unionize for a number of reasons. The June 1995 election of Mike Harris's Conservative government in Ontario filled university workers with a sense of insecurity, given the government's aggressive cost-cutting agenda, and unionization was seen as a way of protecting job security. In addition, the university administration had made a series of arbitrary policy decisions in the areas of workload and discipline, prompting university professors to seek formal legal recognition in the form of a union. A faculty association had existed for years, but unionization granted it additional legal powers. As association President Dawn Good explained at the time, winning certification would ensure that faculty members could protect their gains and be "equal partners" in education.[15]

In 1998, part-time instructors, teaching assistants, lab demonstrators, and marker-graders followed the lead of faculty members and voted in favour of union representation. These university workers, who were among the lowest paid in Canada, opted to join CUPE. The university's administrative staff, after failed attempts at unionization in 1998 and 2000, finally won union certification in 2002. This group of university workers opted to join the Ontario Secondary School Teachers Federation (OSSTF) and, in the process, helped the union break into new territory.

Heidi Klose, an administrative assistant in the Department of History at Brock University, recounted her experience with unionization:

> There have been a number of attempts to organize staff at Brock University over many years. My involvement began in 1998 when I led a drive with another union. The reason I took part in this endeavour was because the teaching assistants were in the planning stages of their organizing attempt. I was convinced, because our TAs had the lowest wages in the province, that their campaign would be successful and so it was. Brock faculty, who for many years were members of a faculty association, had one year earlier seen the wisdom of forming an actual union. Trades people, cleaners and food employees, even the parking-lot attendants had their own union. This meant that the support staff here at Brock would be the only employee group without any representation. Not only did we not have the protection of a union, but we also had no voice in issues that were most important to us. We would, as always, get the scraps, so to speak, of what was left over in the budget after the administration had negotiated with all the unions.

During the 1998 union drive, our organizing committee consisted of eight people who worked very hard. Evidence that we had a lot of support was in the number of cards that were signed and we had a large verbal commitment as well. In the end, however, we felt that this was not enough for a strong majority vote. There was another drive with the same union two years later; one in which I was not involved. During this campaign the organizing committee felt that the support needed from the union was not there. The campaign fizzled out and many union supporters, as well as the organizing committees for these two campaigns, became disillusioned.

We were not even thinking of another drive when a colleague of mine, Virginia Wagg, and I were informed by another colleague that someone from OSSTF was interested in organizing Brock staff members. We had never even considered contacting this union because we thought that they represented only high school teachers. Shirley Dufour, organizer for OSSTF, met with two of my colleagues and asked if others would be interested in attending an information meeting. Shirley had anticipated five or six people but when word got out, about 20 enthusiastic people showed up. Shirley spoke about OSSTF and how professional they were and we were hooked. A vote was taken and the decision was unanimous that we would begin a drive right then and there.

There really was no formal organizing committee per se, but everyone who had attended the meeting did their part in getting others to sign cards or encourage people to come to one of three information sessions.

Lo and behold in a very short time we had enough cards signed. That was the difference with the other drives; they always took so long and just petered out. We made an application to the Labour Board and were granted a vote. Just getting to this stage was a huge success, but things would get even better. Virginia volunteered to be our scrutineer. I was both amazed and proud that she had the courage to put her name forward and then sit in the polling station for an entire day knowing that someone from Human Resources would be there as well. With great anticipation, Shirley, Virginia and I, along with others from Human Resources, watched after the poll closed to see the ballots being counted. And sure enough we had won with a great majority. I wasn't surprised because I knew how strong the union support was within our group. I know that with a bit of patience and a lot of hard work, we can improve our working conditions at Brock. We are the first university staff members to be organized by OSSTF and so it will be both a challenge and a tremendous opportunity. We have great expectations.[16]

In 2009, CUPE organized English as a Second Language coordinators at Brock and went on to win substantial improvements in terms of job security for these workers. As of May 2011, the overwhelming majority of workers at Brock University — including professors, librarians, teaching assistants, cafeteria workers, administrative assistants, and maintenance, custodial, and clerical workers — belong to labour unions. Indeed, there are five separate union locals on campus, representing roughly two thousand workers. The high level of union density at Brock University, which reflects the high levels of unionization in the public post-secondary sector as a whole, stands in stark contrast to the steep decline in unionization that unions in Niagara, and across Canada, have witnessed in the private sector, particularly in manufacturing.

## Living in a Dying Town: Deindustrialization in Welland

On 2 September 2008, company executives from farm equipment manufacturer John Deere called a mandatory meeting for all of the Welland Works employees at the company's Dain City plant in Welland. CAW union local president Tom Napper described what happened next:

There were 800 people standing in one of the warehouse-type things with speakers set up, and they brought in the manager and they brought in one of the big guys from the States, and they proceeded to let our manager make the announcement that we are here today to announce the closure of John Deere Welland Works, and that was how they opened and closed . . . it was short and sweet. I would have to say that's probably one of the worst predicaments I've witnessed, to look across the room at people that I've worked with for 30 years and plus, and their chins actually hit the pavement. As a matter of fact, most people just turned and said, "What . . . what . . . what did he say? I couldn't have heard that right."

They were astonished because actually the mood in the plant . . . they thought that they were going to be there for an announcement to maybe add another product . . . because they had been so busy, they were just working seven days a week, they were behind schedule, everything was good.[1]

Since the late 1980s, the Niagara region, following the national trend, has experienced steep declines in the rate of private sector unionization. Nowhere has that trend been more apparent than in the industrial, blue-collar city of Welland. For the past several decades, Welland has seen its base of heavily unionized industry steadily eroded through a combination of irresponsible management, unfriendly government policy, and a reckless free market. Between 1991 and 2001, the city lost roughly six thousand manufacturing jobs (both union and non-union) through plant closures and corporate downsizing.[2]

Despite the fact that the industrial sector in Welland had been suffering for several decades, having never really recovered from the deindustrialization precipitated by the introduction of free trade in the late 1980s, the announced closure of the John Deere plant in many ways defied logic. After all, the company was profitable, the product was in demand, and the workforce was both reliable and efficient. Over the years, when the company and the union entered into contract talks, management would frequently raise the spectre of plant closure in an effort to gain the upper hand in collective bargaining. But the union was certainly not prepared for an actual plant closure. Indeed, the announcement caught workers completely off guard.

For its part, the company told the local media that "the decision is not a reflection of the work or productivity of our employees."[3] Instead, John Deere blamed the high exchange rate and soaring energy costs. The bottom line, however, was that the company was motivated by greed. It knew it could make more money by closing its profitable Welland plant and opening a new plant in Mexico operated by workers who would earn a fraction of what the company's Canadian workers were making. The announced closure of the John Deere plant in Welland sent shock waves through the community and generated national headlines as a stark example of the crisis in deindustrialization facing Canadian workers and their communities.

Because John Deere workers earned and spent millions of dollars a year, from which local small businesses benefitted, the negative economic impact of the job loss was felt throughout the community and inevitably caused more business closures and layoffs in Welland.[4] On top of growing unemployment, social service organizations noted increased demand at local foodbanks, while local charitable organizations struggled to reach fundraising goals owing to the shrinking amounts of disposable income available to the jobless and to workers who feared joblessness just around the corner. The wider community also suffered as a result of a severely eroded tax base. The taxes John Deere employees paid on the money they earned was used to fund community infrastructure and social programs, and both suffered as a result of the plant closure. In short, when John Deere workers lost their jobs, the entire community lost out. In 2009, the CLC published a "communities in crisis" report, which featured Welland as a case study. In it, Rosina Bisci, a local elementary school teacher interviewed as part of the study, observed that "empty plants, just like monuments to another era, are now just sad reminders of what's happening."[5]

In the wake of the company's devastating decision to close the Welland plant, a sardonic twist on the company's well-known slogan, "Nothing runs (away) like a Deere," became a popular turn of phrase among locals.[6] Tapping into the sense of anger, fear, and frustration in the community, Mark Lammert, a Niagara College student filmmaker, decided to chronicle the fallout from the plant closure in *Dear John*, a documentary that also served as a school project.[7] Lammert interviewed John Deere workers about the impact of the plant closure on their lives, their families, and their sense of self. Lammert had not set out to take sides when he began production, but the company's decision to avoid his phone calls and ignore his emails prompted him to travel to John Deere's corporate headquarters in Moline, Illinois, in search of answers. After the company refused to meet with him in Moline, Lammert, armed with an oversized community greeting card signed by hundreds of concerned residents, held a press conference to talk about what he had learned during his trek to Illinois. Needless to say, he was unimpressed with the actions of John Deere. "I don't think it looks good on their part. I didn't want to look biased or slanted, but it's kind of hard to not make them look like this big bad corporation when they won't even sit down with me," he told the media.[8] *Dear John* was screened at the Canadian Labour International Film Festival in 2009 and won a number of prizes at film festivals across the country in 2010.[9]

CAW chief economist Jim Stanford was featured in the documentary and explained the impact of deindustrialization as follows:

The loss of manufacturing jobs is more than just the individuals who have lost their jobs. Obviously, it's a tragedy for them and their families to have their livelihoods disappear, but it's also a tragedy for our communities. Manufacturing is the most important part of Ontario's economic base. Those are the industries where we produce things that people elsewhere in the world want to buy.

And then, on top of that base, the other jobs in our community depend on the base being there. Things like dry cleaners, or restaurants, or coffee shops — private services. Even public services, like schools and hospitals, depend on us having a strong manufacturing foundation. Otherwise there is nobody there to pay the taxes that support those other jobs. So, for every job that is lost in manufacturing, there are three or four or five jobs elsewhere in the economy that also disappear. That is why our entire community is at stake here.[10]

The announcement of the John Deere plant closure, having gained national prominence, became a central local issue in the 2008 federal election campaign. CAW National President Buzz Hargrove blamed the plant closure on the federal government led by Conservative Stephen Harper. "This government's utter insensitivity to the plight of working Canadians is shameful and must come to an end. . . . In my 16 years as president of the union, I have never seen such governmental indifference," he told the media.[11] Industry officials like Jay Myers, president of the Canadian Manufacturers and Exporters, also pointed the finger at Ottawa. Myers told the media that "to some extent, the government is looking at the economy through rose-coloured glasses. . . . If we don't do more to save manufacturing, we'll have lost a lot of high-paying jobs and value-added industrial companies."[12]

Prime Minister Harper visited Welland during the campaign, but his decision to stay silent on the plant closure, in favour of a policy announcement concerning the regulation of flavoured cigarettes, left a bitter taste in the mouths of many city residents, especially the workers facing job loss at John Deere.[13] The policy announcement made the prime minister appear to be out of touch with the most pressing issues facing the community and, in part, helped deliver the riding to the NDP for the first time in history.

Welland NDP candidate Malcolm Allen (*left*) and NDP leader Jack Layton (*right*) host a press conference in front of the John Deere plant in Welland as part of the 2008 federal election campaign. Courtesy of the New Democratic Party.

During the campaign, NDP candidate Malcolm Allen, a CAW member and deputy mayor of Pelham, lambasted successive Liberal and Conservative governments for providing companies like John Deere with huge corporate tax cuts without any guarantees of job security for workers. Allen and NDP leader Jack Layton held a press conference outside the plant during the campaign to highlight the plight of the workers and criticize the federal government's failure to take action to combat deindustrialization. Allen and Layton blamed the plant closure on continental free trade and the federal government's lack of an industrial policy. Their message resonated. On election day, Allen narrowly defeated his Conservative rival by roughly three hundred votes and also bested longtime Liberal MP John Maloney, whose party had campaigned hard against free trade while in opposition but had embraced the policy once the Liberals formed the government in 1993.

"We just let industries walk in and walk out with no regard for what it means for communities, for workers and ultimately for the Canadian economy in general," said the newly minted Welland MP after his election. "That's a travesty and that needs to stop," he told the local media.[14] During his first week in Ottawa, Allen raised the issue of the plant closure in the House of Commons. He is quoted in the 24 November 2008 edition of *Hansard*:

John Deere had been in the city of Welland for close to 100 years. By its own admission it was highly profitable and highly efficient, with a great workforce. It said in a statement it issued last year that it had a commitment to Welland, yet within nine months it made another announcement to the effect that it was closing the door without any discussions with anyone. It did not even say thank you very much for the tax cuts before moving on.

I talked to a young couple. The husband worked at John Deere. They were in their late twenties or early thirties, not much older than my own children. They told me they had thought they had finally found a secure job in [the Niagara region], because John Deere was the shining star of the region. When all the other manufacturers were losing jobs, this one was actually hiring. What I saw on their faces was desperation. They were asking me, "What will we do? Where do we go next? What will become of us, our friends and our families when we have to leave?"

It is absolutely heart-wrenching to see a young family in that situation, wanting to stay in their community and to be close to their family. They want to raise their children so that the grandparents will have the opportunity to see those grandchildren. They are looking to us in this House to find ways for them to stay in their community by creating jobs for them and not letting them disappear, and not letting the John Deeres take the corporate tax cuts the Conservatives are giving them and head south to Mexico.[15]

There is a broad consensus that the manufacturing jobs lost in Welland are unlikely to ever come back. While some of the city's leaders have proposed alternative plans for local economic development, the case of Welland demonstrates all too well the problem of allowing a community to become hostage to a callous and indifferent free market system that allows companies to treat workers and their communities as expendable vessels in the unapologetic pursuit of profit.

# "Kicking Ass for the Working Class": Hotel Workers in Niagara

Although Niagara Falls has always been a popular tourist destination, the city's local economy relied primarily on manufacturing from the early 1900s well into the post-war period. While the Welland Canal facilitated industrial expansion in St. Catharines, Welland, Thorold, and Port Colborne, it was the advent of cheap hydroelectric power that spurred the development of industry in Niagara Falls, with industrial unions following shortly thereafter.

When the Niagara Falls and District Labour Council was founded in 1956, it comprised eighteen affiliated union locals representing approximately three thousand members.[1] At its peak in the mid-1970s, the Labour Council represented roughly ten thousand members through twenty-nine affiliated unions — the largest being CUPE Local 1000, which represented five hundred workers at Ontario Hydro.[2] The Labour Council played a key advocacy role for unemployed workers and injured workers, had representatives on a variety of city committees, and worked closely with community groups like the United Way in order to improve the lives of working people. It provided financial assistance to various charities and presented briefs to City Council on matters of both local and national importance. Its most impressive achievement was the development of the Niagara Falls Unemployed Help Centre in the early 1980s.

The advent of free trade hit the industrial sector in Niagara Falls particularly hard in the late 1980s. The Ford Glass plant, Gerber, Cyanamid, the Norton Company, and Chef Boyardee all closed their doors and headed south, leaving thousands of local workers unemployed. While industrial unions pushed for tougher plant closure laws that would yield better separation benefits for workers, they also looked to the tourism industry as an area of potential growth. The hotel and hospitality industry in Niagara Falls, although long-standing, was barely unionized. The seasonal and casual nature of the industry, coupled with the limited number of workers in each potential bargaining unit, rendered organizing difficult. Although Local 442 of the Hotel, Motel and Restaurant Employees Union (HERE) had been representing workers in Niagara Falls since 1942, the union was quite small and represented only a relatively minor fraction of tourism workers, rendering it weak at the bargaining table.

In April 1993, local businessman Dino DiCienzo gained control of a significant portion of the city's hotel industry by purchasing a group of three prominent hotels in the Clifton Hill tourist area: the Skyline Brock, the Foxhead, and the Village Inn.[3] Along with the new hotels, DiCienzo inherited about two hundred union members who worked at the hotels — all members of HERE Local 442. Labour relations between the union and the previous hotel owners had been quite harmonious. In fact, longtime Local 442 President James Whyte told the *Niagara Falls Review* that the hotels had not experienced a strike since 1940.[4] However, all of this was about to change dramatically.

DiCienzo's new group of hotels, operating as Canadian Niagara Hotels, received a major boost when the provincial government decided to open a temporary casino in the Clifton Hill tourist area. Not only were all three hotel properties adjacent to the proposed site for the casino, but DiCienzo also owned the land where the casino was eventually built and thus became the operation's landlord. In anticipation of the opening of Casino Niagara in 1996, DiCienzo invested heavily in upgrading and expanding his hotel empire through the addition of a food court and a Hard Rock Café directly adjacent to Casino Niagara. This expansion indirectly benefitted Local 442 because it required the company to hire more employees, thus potentially swelling the ranks of the union. However, when Canadian Niagara Hotels opened the Terrace Food Court and the Hard Rock Café in December 1996, the company made it clear that it preferred to operate non-union when it rebuffed Local 442's attempt to assert bargaining rights for the company's newest workers. Local 442 argued that the scope clause in its collective agreement with Canadian Niagara Hotels covered all employees of the company within the City of Niagara Falls, but the company argued that the union's contract only covered employees working in the existing hotels.[5] Unable to resolve the dispute, Local 442 threatened legal action at the OLRB. Faced with no reasonable prospect of winning the eventual legal challenge at the board, Canadian Niagara Hotels begrudgingly recognized the union as the bargaining agent for workers at both the Terrace Food Court and the Hard Rock Café. The episode contributed to the creation of a chilly relationship between a fledgling labour union seeking to expand its clout and a growing company that saw the union as an impediment to the maximization of profit.

Relations between the union and the company became strained over the course of the next few years. In September 1998, Local 442 merged with its much bigger Toronto-based sister, HERE Local 75, which represented workers at a number of large and prominent hotels in that city, including the Royal York. The leadership of Local 442 argued that, in order to combat an increasingly hostile employer, it needed the additional resources that only a bigger union could bring to the table.[6]

In October 1999, Local 75 entered into collective bargaining with Canadian Niagara Hotels. The increased size of the hotels had bolstered the size of the union, which had grown to roughly six hundred members, including room attendants, kitchen and restaurant staff, valet attendants, food court attendants, and front desk workers. Talks between the union and management broke down on 3 December 1999. A failed round of conciliation set the stage for a "no board" report, placing the union in a legal strike position and the employer in a legal lockout position as of 23 December 1999.

While reservation and front desk staff successfully concluded their collective agreement by a vote of 22 to 13 on 14 December 1999, other workers in the hotel were unwilling to settle for the management's final offer, which included a proposal to split off the Terrace Food Court and the Hard Rock Café from the hotels, offering a one-year agreement for the latter worksites and a three-year agreement for the former.[7] Recognizing the danger of management's divide-and-conquer strategy, the union steadfastly refused to accept any proposal that would divide the workers by worksite. The workers rejected the final offer by a margin of 286 to 23, thus setting the stage for the first strike in the history of Canadian Niagara Hotels. The union chose 23 December 1999 as the strike deadline date. However, because winter is the down season for tourism in Niagara Falls, the union was not in a very strong position to hurt the company's bottom line with a prolonged strike. The union therefore announced that it would organize 24-hour rotating strikes on December 28 and on New Year's Eve, a particularly busy time at the hotels amid a slow winter season.

In response, management threatened a lockout — a rare tactic in the hospitality industry — and began organizing buses to transport replacement workers across union picket lines in the event of a prolonged strike.[8] With tensions high, the union stepped up its response, organizing a demonstration on Falls Avenue in front of the Skyline Brock hotel on 18 December 1999. Hotel workers and their community allies marched and waved placards, while members of senior management observed the demonstration from the hotel's elevated lobby window. Local MPP Peter Kormos addressed the picketers, declaring "It's about bloody time you got to share in these new huge profits."[9]

On 22 December 1999, both management and union negotiators met late into the night in a last-ditch attempt to resolve the dispute. In the early hours of 23 December 1999, both sides secured a three-year agreement that included wage increases and an improved benefits package. Most importantly, for the union, management backed away from its proposal to sever the bargaining unit so as to divide workers by worksite. The agreement was later ratified by union members by a vote of 260 to 19.[10]

Shortly after the contract was ratified, front desk and reservation staff at the hotels — many of whom identified more closely with management than with the room attendants and kitchen staff who provided the most solid support for the union — decertified Local 75. The union complained that hotel management had initiated the decertification campaign and expressed concern that members of the hotel management team were planning to work closely with a handful of anti-union employees to decertify the remaining bargaining units, one by one.[11] The union also complained that Canadian Niagara Hotels carried on business as if Local 75 did not even exist. Hotel management selectively applied provisions of the collective agreement, dismissed grievances out of hand, and targeted anyone who became active in the union. Management's refusal to recognize the union's legitimacy made it very difficult for Local 75 to justify its existence and thus build support among workers.

In November 2000, the anti-union provincial Conservative government introduced new legislation that required employers to post information in unionized workplaces on how to decertify a union. While the minister of Labour defended the legislation by arguing that the provincial government was simply informing workers of their rights, critics of the provincial government challenged his logic, arguing that the government's position was hypocritical. "He is going to be posting in workplaces for employees who are unionized how to decertify, yet he will not be posting in a non-unionized location, how to certify," complained Leah Casselman, president of the Ontario Public Service Employees Union (OPSEU).[12] In October

2002, three months before the expiry of the collective agreement negotiated in December 1999, anti-union workers, assisted by management, began circulating a petition to decertify Local 75.[13] Once 40 percent of the workers had signed the petition to decertify the union, the OLRB conducted a workplace vote by secret ballot to determine the union's fate. In a resounding show of support for the union, workers voted 359 to 96 in favour of keeping Local 75 as its bargaining agent.[14]

On 21 November 2002, members of Local 75 voted 69 percent in favour of rejecting management's final offer and authorizing a strike.[15] The final offer included yet another proposal to divide workers by worksite through the creation of three separate bargaining units: one for the hotels, one for the Hard Rock Café, and a third for the Terrace Food Court. Management's union-busting strategy was based on the knowledge that workers at the Hard Rock Café and the Terrace Food Court were more likely to support efforts to decertify the union. Separating these two worksites from the comparatively larger hotel bargaining unit — where the union enjoyed overwhelming support — would weaken the union and thus make the task of decertifying the union easier to accomplish.

On 1 December 2002, Local 75 moved into a legal strike position. Three days later, hotel management fired two of the union's five bargaining team members. In response, the union took to the streets on 6 December 2002 in what the *Niagara Falls Review* called "one of the first strikes in the history of Niagara Falls tourism."[16] Workers carried signs reading, "All we want for Christmas is a fair contract" and chanted, "I don't know if you've been told, DiCienzo's made of gold."[17] However, a significant number of workers crossed the picket line, prompting Gord Arbeau, director of marketing for Canadian Niagara Hotels, to tell local media, "We've proven that we can run business as usual, and I think that's strengthened our resolve."[18]

The company retaliated by cancelling the shifts of some of the workers who had participated in the one-day picket or had respected the picket lines. In response, the union filed unfair labour practice complaints against the company, charging that there had been over a hundred individual cases of retaliation against pro-union employees.[19] The union also set up a cyber picket line in the form of a website that encouraged the public to avoid patronizing establishments in the Clifton Hill area owned by Canadian Niagara Hotels.[20] At the hotel, rumours swirled that hotel management, anticipating a long, drawn-out labour dispute, had already lined up replacement workers and had cleared several floors' worth of rooms to house them for the duration of the strike so that they would not have to cross hostile picket lines.[21]

In the end, the replacement workers were not needed. On 13 and 14 December 2002, members of Local 75 voted 258 to 256 in favour of a second final offer from management, which came the day after the union's one-day picket on 6 December. The offer provided slightly greater financial incentives, including a wage increase of 9 percent over three years. However, it retained the controversial union-busting provision to divide workers into multiple bargaining units, thereby inevitably setting the stage for future decertification attempts. The agreement also mandated a process of final offer selection for the next round of collective bargaining, which would prevent the parties involved from engaging in a strike or a lockout to settle the next contract. Instead, an arbitrator would choose between final offers made by the company and by the union. This second offer was ratified, although by a very narrow margin, despite the fact that the union's bargaining team did not recommend support. Local 75 president Paul Clifford told the *Niagara Falls Review*: "I believe that the vote was more about the ability of relatively moderate income workers to sustain a long, protracted labour dispute."[22]

Despite the settlement, or perhaps because of it, tension between the union and Canadian Niagara Hotels remained high. Nearly a year later, in October 2003, Local 75 member Kim McQuillan, a banquet server at the Sheraton on the Falls, delivered a speech to a gathering of steelworkers who were holding a conference at the hotel. The steelworkers had heard about Local 75's recent disputes with hotel management and invited McQuillan to shed some light on the situation. In her speech, McQuillan described the union's prolonged struggle with Canadian Niagara Hotels, including the company's recent attempts to decertify the union. She told the assembled steelworkers that her employer was a "powerhouse of profit" and explained that "money was no object to them in fighting to get rid of the union." [23] Unimpressed by McQuillan's speech, hotel management ushered her into a disciplinary meeting. She was later suspended without pay until she agreed to retract her speech and write a letter of apology. Unrepentant, McQuillan refused to apologize, and Local 75 filed a grievance against hotel management, insisting that union members were entitled to free speech. In response, the hotel's owner launched a defamation lawsuit against McQuillan and the union officials who had helped her craft the speech.[24]

Amid all the controversy and heightened labour-management tension, the union lost significant support in the workplace. Some of the workers who had participated in the rotating strikes in December 2002 complained that the union had caved in too easily, while others were upset that the union had initiated the strikes in the first place. In the wake of the labour dispute, Canadian Niagara Hotels was emboldened in its efforts to break the union. As a result, in July 2004, workers at the Hard Rock Café and the Terrace Food Court voted 57 to 34 to decertify Local 75.[25]

Three years later, in July 2007, the Ontario Superior Court of Justice dismissed the defamation case against McQuillan, much to the delight of the union and its allies. In his decision, Justice Thomas Lederer ruled that the dispute arose directly from the employment relationship and that suing McQuillan and the union officials constituted "an improper attempt to remove the dispute to the court only after the Company's efforts to obtain an apology through its authority, under the collective agreement, to discipline [had] failed."[26] Wayne Fraser, of the steelworkers, issued a press release after the decision, explaining that "our members were inspired by McQuillan's speech to our convention and . . . were shocked when Canadian Niagara Hotels and its ownership chose to discipline, then discharge and finally launch this action against her and officials from her union. We are very happy to see this action dismissed." [27]

In 2004, HERE merged with UNITE (the Union of Needletrades, Industrial and Textile Employees) to form UNITE HERE. In Niagara, the bargaining units of both former unions became Local 2347, a composite local covering all of Niagara. In addition to workers at Canadian Niagara Hotels, Local 2347 represented servers at Niagara Parks, food and beverage staff at the Fort Erie Racetrack, restaurant workers and groundskeepers at the St. Catharines Golf and Country Club, and workers at Filerfab, a small manufacturer based in St. Catharines. The change in unions notwithstanding, labour relations between the local and the management of Canadian Niagara Hotels remained sour. [28] A few months before the expiry of the collective agreement, a company-initiated petition to decertify the union started to make its way around the workplace. Having anticipated this employer offensive, the union had been preparing workers for the decertification vote that was on the horizon. In the end, much to the dismay of hotel management, the union won the vote soundly. Union organizers reasoned that the employer's aggressive anti-union approach had backfired — only reconfirming for workers why they needed a union. Despite its victory in the decertification campaign, the union entered into contract negotiations with Canadian Niagara Hotels with a bitter taste in its mouth.

When negotiations predictably arrived at an impasse, an arbitrator was called in to settle the dispute, as part of the final offer selection process the parties had agreed to in the previous collective agreement. Assuming the company would go overboard in its final offer, given its rabidly anti-union approach to labour relations, the union strategically submitted a final offer that contained meaningful but not ground-breaking demands. The union's strategy paid off when arbitrator Bill Kaplan ultimately chose Local 2347's final proposal over hotel management's. The new collective agreement included free parking for employees, guaranteed eight-hour shifts, and workload reduction for room attendants, as well as a 9 percent wage increase over three years. The agreement also included provisions for a $100 bonus for each employee upon ratification of the contract. However, as soon as the ink was dry on the new collective agreement, trouble began to brew between hotel management and the union.

Annoyed that the arbitrator had chosen the union's final proposal over its own, and determined to undermine the union's legitimacy in the workplace, hotel management withheld the bonus that had been negotiated in the contract. It also implemented a split-shift system designed to encourage room attendants to forgo their right to a standard eight-hour day.[29] Hotel management, it seemed, was hell-bent on busting the union.

On 16 September 2006, well-known actor Danny Glover traveled to Niagara Falls to attend a union rally in support of the workers employed by Canadian Niagara Hotels. Dubbed "labour's lethal weapon" by local media — a reference to his starring role alongside Mel Gibson in the *Lethal Weapon* films — Glover was speaking at union rallies all across North America in support of hotel workers. The actor was lending his celebrity to the cause of organized labour because, in his own words, "the unions are in the perfect position to be the anti-poverty program in the 21st century."[30] Glover joined the demonstration deep in the city's tourism district and listened intently as hotel workers took turns at a megaphone describing the climate of workplace intimidation at the hotels. Michelle Hemmingson, a room attendant, spoke at the rally during her lunch break. "Despite the fact we won a great new contract, hotel management has mostly ignored it," she declared.[31] Glover's presence at the rally, which took over a stretch of Falls Avenue directly in front of the Sheraton on the Falls hotel, piqued the interest of tourists, who posed for pictures with the Hollywood star and cheered him on as he spoke in defence of local hotel workers.

Actor Danny Glover addresses hotel workers and their allies at a demonstration against Canadian Niagara Hotels in Niagara Falls on 16 September 2006. Courtesy of UNITE HERE.

Glover told the demonstrators and a growing crowd of tourists that the union's fight for dignity and respect was just and that the hotel workers had his full support. After his impassioned speech, he joined union president Alex Dagg and OFL president Wayne Samuelson in an attempt to confront hotel management over the treatment of the hotel's workers. The trio entered the lobby of the Sheraton on the Falls and demanded to speak with the management about the outstanding grievances and the complaints against the hotel that had been filed with the OLRB. But management declined to engage them. According to hotel security, the trio were repeatedly asked to leave the lobby but refused, prompting a call to the Niagara Regional Police. The hotel asked the police to arrest Glover, Dagg, and Samuelson for trespassing, but the police were unwilling to lay charges. A sergeant later explained to local media that "everyone was co-operative and Mr. Glover was a gentleman throughout the event." [32]

When the trio left the hotel lobby and announced to the crowd that management had refused to meet with them, demonstrators booed and jeered. "We're going to keep coming back until we have the opportunity to meet with the owners of this hotel. And I don't care how many times it takes us and we're going to bring more people out next time," exclaimed Dagg, much to the approval of the crowd.[33]

Enraged by the union's tactics, Canadian Niagara Hotels decided to pursue private prosecutions against Glover, Dagg, and Samuelson. The charge against Glover had the effect of focusing major media attention on the dispute. Glover explained his participation in the rally as follows: "I was using the presence and visibility I have to bring attention to the cause and to get the owners adhering to the contract they signed."[34] His trespass charge and his support for the union became national news.

In response to Canadian Niagara Hotel's decision to pursue private prosecution, union members from across Ontario met in Niagara Falls on the evening of 13 December 2006 for another demonstration against the company. Hotel workers were flanked by members of the CAW, USWA, OPSEU, and an assortment of other unions, all waving flags and carrying picket signs calling for workplace justice at Canadian Niagara Hotels. Dagg told the assembled crowd that, in addition to taking legal action against Glover, Dagg, and Samuelson, hotel management was refusing to pay out the $100 signing bonus the union had won for members in the last round of collective bargaining. The union was also demanding the implementation of an eight-hour work day without split shifts.[35] From the corner of Lorne and Centre streets, above the Clifton Hill tourist area, union members and their community allies marched through the city, chanting and waving union flags, en route to the Sheraton on the Falls.

Once demonstrators reached the rally point, across from the hotel, the children of several hotel workers addressed the crowd, describing the negative impact of the hotel's split-shift policy on their family life. Dagg explained that the "newly implemented split shifts are forcing our members to make a horrible choice between being able to work enough hours to support their families or spending time with their families."[36] As for the contested $100 signing bonus, Dagg pointed out that it "could go a long way towards buying presents for the kids this Christmas."[37] As she went on to argue: "The company doesn't need to do split shifts or withhold the bonus. At this time of year, especially, people want to know they can spend time with their kids and give them a good Christmas. At this rate, I wouldn't be surprised if some of the folks in the management of this company were visited by three ghosts this Christmas Eve."[38]

A union activist dressed in a Santa Claus costume injected some humour into the gathering. "My elves have been collecting documentation on the activities of this hotel company," he told the assembled hotel workers and their families. "So far it doesn't look very good for the company. I fear that I may have to give them a lump of coal this Christmas."[39] At this point, a union supporter, who had covertly checked into the hotel earlier that day, unfurled a large banner from the window of a room directly overlooking the rally point. The banner read: "DON'T LET THE GRINCH STEAL CHRISTMAS! TELL CANADIAN NIAGARA HOTELS: STOP THE WAR ON WORKING FAMILIES." The unveiling of the banner sent hotel security into a mad scramble, while demonstrators cheered.[40]

The next day, Local 2347 revealed that just prior to the start of its holiday-themed demonstration, hotel management had sent a fax to the union's headquarters threatening to rescind a wage increase for banquet servers. The union responded by issuing a press release, calling the company's move a "thinly veiled attempt to intimidate the union and workers from exercising their democratic right to free speech."[41]

Meanwhile, the company's lawsuit against Glover, Dagg, and Samuelson in connection with the alleged trespass incident of 16 September was making its way through the legal system. Frank Addario, the lawyer defending the trio, officially announced that all three would plead not guilty to the charge. Addario also served notice that he would be challenging the constitutional validity of the company's private prosecution.

Glover's central role in the legal battle significantly boosted the union's profile and inspired hotel workers like Michelle Hemmingson to stand up and be counted. However, given the level of animosity between hotel management and the union, new rank-and-file activists became a prime target for employer intimidation. In April 2007, Hemmingson was fired for allegedly stealing from the company — one of a number of union activists discharged by hotel management. The union subsequently filed a grievance against the hotel, arguing that the firing was unjustified and was motivated solely by Hemmingson's emergence as a strong supporter of the union.

At the same time, the union invited Hemmingson to address meetings of union members across Niagara and Hamilton to raise awareness about Canadian Niagara Hotel's campaign against union activists. Speaking to the St. Catharines and District Labour Council, Hemmingson described the history of the dispute and underscored the need for solidarity:

> My name is Michelle Hemmingson. . . . I worked at one of the three hotels owned by Canadian Niagara Hotels, otherwise known as C.N.H. . . . These are big hotels. At the Sheraton alone, there are 670 rooms in a hotel that directly faces the falls. These rooms start at about $150 a night and go up to $500. Even in the slow season, these hotels are busy. Besides facing the falls, they are also connected to the Niagara Casino. The casino even pays rent to C.N.H. for the land upon which the casino sits, to the tune of $2.2 million a month. With all this money coming in, you would think that the hotel owners would be interested in treating their employees right. I am here to tell you a bit about my story and to call on you to join my fellow workers in trying to make C.N.H. respect the contract of my unionized brothers and sisters. . . .
>
> . . . Who are we? Generally, people who work in the hotel industry in Niagara Falls are women or young people. It used to be that these people were earning a second income for the family. The

other family member worked in the higher paying stable manufacturing jobs. With the decline of the manufacturing sector, more and more families in Niagara Falls are finding themselves with having to support their children on one or two hotel jobs. It's a tough struggle, but we do it.

I began my time at C.N.H. three years ago and used the money to support my son, Cole, and myself. At first I kept my head down and kept to myself. After a time, though, I began to really dislike what I saw happening around the hotel. I didn't like the way I saw people being treated, and I felt I needed to do something. I got involved in the union and eventually became shop steward.

Things came to a head in 2005 with the most recent set of contract negotiations. Negotiations dragged on and on until eventually, at management's request, we went to final contract selection. This is a rarely used bit of labour law that says that both sides write up their best offer and give them to the arbitrator. The arbitrator then picks one or the other. The company's proposal was so outlandish that the arbitrator chose our version of the contract.

There were a couple of key changes in the union's proposal. The life of a room attendant is measured by the number of rooms you have to clean in a shift. It's a lot of work to clean a room. You have to vacuum the floor, strip the bed, replace linens and towels, clean the bathroom, wash toilets, and replace various amenities, as well as [perform] other tasks depending on the standards of the hotel. At C.N.H., with the old standard of sixteen rooms in an eight-hour shift, that's half an hour per room. Notice that is with no breaks. We are always hurrying or having to work off the clock. This results in people getting hurt or having to sacrifice family time for work.

In the new contract, we won a reduction in the number of rooms required to be cleaned per shift from sixteen to fifteen. A small reduction but significant in this town with only 6 percent union density. We also won a salary increase of 3 percent for each of the three years of the contract. Again, very significant to people who are working pay cheque to pay cheque.

On top of the low pay per hour, there is the battle to get hours.

We won a provision that required the employer to give people full eight-hour shifts rather than the six-hour shifts that were standard previously. This increased our hours per week from thirty to forty. Again, a significant matter of money. We had hoped that with the increase in hours there would be less need for us to work second jobs.

There were a few other improvements, but I won't go into details because really, none of that matters. In my opinion, C.N.H. has been trying to steal as much power away from their employees as possible. I see this as part of a long-term campaign to push the union out of the hotel.

Those eight-hour shifts I was just speaking about? C.N.H. decided they would schedule people for eight-hour shifts, but they were split shifts. This means that people would come in and work for six or seven hours, be told to get off the property for two or three hours, and [then] come back for the remaining one or two hours. Can you imagine that? In the interest of working ten more hours a week, you end up spending ten to twenty hours waiting. And there is little business sense in using split shifts for room attendants in a hotel. At 7:00 p.m. at night, there is little work for them to do. In my opinion, this wasn't about business sense; it was about getting people to give in.

C.N.H. offered people "an out." They could sign away their right to an eight-hour shift, and they would just be scheduled for a six-hour shift. The pressures of life outside of work forced almost every room attendant to do just that. We gave up our right to ten more hours per week because our boss didn't want to accept the terms of the contract. Think about it for a minute. These ten hours represent $480 in salary for a room attendant. . . .

. . . Even on the simple matter of the award bonus, C.N.H. has been stubborn. According to the contract, they were to pay out a $100 bonus for the awarding of the contract. Again, delay, delay, delay. It's been eleven months since the contract was awarded, and they still haven't paid it out. We're talking about a grand total of about $50,000 here. A small amount for a hotel doing the business that they do. But a large amount for us, the people who keep the hotel running.

As active union members, you are probably thinking, What about grievances? What about filing with the labour board? What about other legal ways of making C.N.H. behave? We are doing all that and more. But all of those processes take time. On top of that, though, when C.N.H. is involved, everything moves extremely slowly. We already have dates for arbitration booked into spring of next year for things that happened last February.

Many people know of the issues that the union and C.N.H. have with each other, but few know what the employees go through on a daily basis. Myself, I have felt continuous pressure since becoming a steward and health and safety activist. It's like walking around with a target on your back. After completing my eight-hour shift, I was held in an investigation meeting for another five hours. I have been suspended for six days.

The numbers speak for themselves. Out of five bargaining committee members that we had in 2005, only one remains working inside the hotel. All health and safety members in the last four years have been fired or have left the workplace on sick leave. The woman that I replaced on the health and safety committee left the hotel in an ambulance because of an anxiety attack and hasn't returned since. Stewards have the same kind of luck at C.N.H., so much [so] that there is only one steward in the entire complex, where our collective agreement says there can be one steward in each department inside each hotel.

Recently, in April, my employment was terminated by C.N.H. because they claimed I had committed an act of theft. I can't say much about the details of my termination as we have filed a grievance that is ongoing. . . .

We don't see C.N.H. complying with many significant parts of the contract, and our union activists have a strange tendency to lose their jobs. They [C.N.H.] are in no risk of going under and are ready to invest their money in several different development projects, and yet I do not see them treating their employees right. It's about time that we demand that this company change its ways.

I would really like to be able to go to work without being afraid.

I would like to be confident that I am going to have a job that will support my family. We all would. That is why I am here today. We are calling on you for solidarity. It is only with community pressure that C.N.H. is going to change their ways.[42]

The labour movement responded to Hemmingson's plea for solidarity. On 16 June 2007, hundreds of labour union activists from across southern Ontario converged on Niagara Falls for yet another demonstration against Canadian Niagara Hotels. The labour march and rally highlighted Hemmingson's unfair firing, with demonstrators carrying picket signs, emblazoned with Hemmingson's image, demanding justice for hotel workers in Niagara. OFL president Wayne Samuelson, who had been charged with trespassing along with Danny Glover and UNITE HERE Canadian Director Alex Dagg in September 2006, returned to Niagara in a show of solidarity with the union, pledging that "the 750,000 members of the labour movement in Ontario will do whatever is necessary to ensure that things change."[43]

Hundreds of union members march in Niagara Falls on 16 June 2007, in support of hotel workers' rights. Courtesy of UNITE HERE.

The demonstrators, who assembled at the corner of Dixon Street and Cleveland Avenue, made their way through the tourism district of Niagara Falls, marching past every single major hotel and both casinos, chanting and beating drums, while tourists and hotel workers on break looked on with interest. Ultimately, the demonstrators stopped in front of the Sheraton on the Falls, where the assembled workers held a noisy rally under the watchful eye of dozens of private security guards hired by the company. Dagg told the assembled crowd, "This hotel has been thumbing their noses at proper standards of employee treatment for years and it has to stop." [44] She went on to explain that "Niagara Falls is a great community and its workers deserve jobs that allow them to support their families and live with dignity. The poor treatment of workers at C.N.H. is a problem for this whole community, especially because so much of the economy is now dependent on tourism." [45] Hemmingson echoed Dagg's comments, arguing that the hotel's poor treatment of its workers "has an effect on our entire community. If Niagara Falls is so dependent on tourism, then we need to make sure jobs in hotels, restaurants and tourist attractions are the types of jobs that allow us and our community to prosper." [46]

The labour movement followed up on 3 September 2007, with a Labour Day rally and march that once again targeted Canadian Niagara Hotels. Local 2347 brought in busloads of members from sister locals across the province to participate in the demonstration. Steelworkers from Hamilton, autoworkers from St. Catharines, teachers, university workers, and other public sector workers from across Niagara swelled the ranks of the participants.

In response, Canadian Niagara Hotels further beefed up its security and videotaped demonstrators as they made their way through the city to the Sheraton on the Falls. The increased level of security was likely due to the presence of Danny Glover at the rally. Even though his trespassing charge was still before the courts, Glover, who was filming a movie a few hours away in Guelph, decided to return to Niagara Falls for the Labour Day rally and march in support of the city's hotel workers. Demonstrators, who had gathered at the corner of Hunter and Union streets, snaked through the city's tourism district waving colourful union flags and carrying banners demanding respect for hotel workers. The leadership of Local 2347 explained that the Labour Day mobilization was motivated by three outstanding issues: the targeting and discharge of union activists, the continued prosecution of Glover, Dagg, and Samuelson for trespass, and the company's ongoing refusal to pay out the contractually negotiated bonus and 3 percent wage increase to banquet staff.[47]

Glover told the assembled crowd that "when men and women organize for better pay, when men and women organize for better working conditions, they're being the best citizens they can be, they're elevating the rest of society. . . . To date, justice has been denied and when justice is denied to one person, it is denied to all."[48] Welland MPP Peter Kormos also spoke at the rally, encouraging hotel workers to stay strong and to keep up the fight.[49]

The union was on a roll. In September 2007, student servers working at the Niagara Parks Commission opted to follow the lead of their full-time counterparts and unionize with Local 2347. The union won 74 percent support in the certification election. In October 2007, arbitrator Howard Brown directed Canadian Niagara Hotels to pay its workers the $100 bonuses that had been negotiated in collective bargaining. In his decision, the arbitrator categorically rejected the company's position on the matter, thus resolving a long-standing dispute between the parties in favour of the union. The union hailed the arbitration decision as a major victory for hotel workers, largely because the non-payment of negotiated bonuses was one of the central issues that had fuelled demonstrations against the company, including the 16 September 2006 rally that resulted in the trespassing lawsuit.[50]

On 30 October 2007, the Ontario Provincial Offences Court in Niagara Falls became a media circus when Danny Glover took the stand to defend himself against Canadian Niagara Hotels' charge that he had trespassed on private property. Frank Addario, the lawyer defending Glover and the union officials, argued that the company's private prosecution had no merit because it violated the freedoms of expression and assembly guaranteed to all Canadians in the Charter of Rights and Freedoms. Addario further argued that the rare private prosecution should not have been used as a substitute for the collective bargaining process.[51] In the end, however, the court was not convinced.

On 24 January 2008, Danny Glover, Alex Dagg, and Wayne Samuelson were convicted of trespassing. "It is sad that even though the police acknowledged everyone was well behaved and did not press charges, a rich and powerful company can pay to go forward with a private prosecution," lamented an unrepentant Alex Dagg.[52] "It raises serious questions for all of us who believe in fairness and equality before the law but it will, in no way, deter us from continuing to stand up for what is right." OFL president Wayne Samuelson reinforced Dagg's view. "The Ontario labour movement will not be deterred by this decision today and will continue to utilize our Charter rights to stand up for working people across this province. It is wrong that those with money can go above the police and purchase a prosecution in this province, and we will stand our ground against such tactics," he said in a press release.[53]

At the sentencing a few weeks later, the trio were fined only $100 each, and Justice of the Peace Moira Moses refused the company's request to force the defendants to foot the bill for private prosecution.[54] Instead, the company would be responsible for paying its own $22,000 legal bill despite its victory in court. Moses characterized the intentions of the three defendants as "noble" and expressed the view that the private prosecution had been unnecessary to protect the interests of the hotel's owners.[55] The defendants took pride in the fact that Moses adopted the position that Canadian Niagara Hotels ought to have engaged in continued good faith negotiations with the union. Moses's ruling amounted to a symbolic victory of sorts for the union and its allies. "It is outrageous that even though our courts are overwhelmed with serious cases and the police refused to charge us for entering the hotel lobby in 2006, this company has wasted its money and the court's time and tax dollars on this matter," Dagg declared. "It is a shame; they could have paid a room attendant for almost a year on the money they've wasted on this."[56] Wayne Samuelson was also mystified by the company's actions, pointing out that the private prosecution of Danny Glover had only drawn more attention to the labour relations problems at the hotels and mobilized even greater numbers of workers against the company.[57]

Local 2347 built on the success of its 2007 Labour Day march against Canadian Niagara Hotels by organizing a second Niagara Falls Labour Day demonstration on 1 September 2008 in conjunction with the Niagara Falls and St. Catharines District Labour Councils. The 2008 Labour Day demonstration was the largest in the history of the city of Niagara Falls. Members of Local 2347, still locked in a prolonged struggle with Canadian Niagara Hotels, wore T-shirts with the slogan "Kicking ass for the working class" and marched behind a banner that read "Niagara Hotel Workers Deserve a Raise." They were joined by the Buffalo chapter of Students Against Sweatshops, a local contingent from the Council of Canadians, a delegation of New Democratic Party activists, and dozens of union locals representing workers in virtually every sector of the economy.[58] Infuriated by Canadian Niagara Hotel's repeated attempts at union-busting, unions and their community allies were determined to send a message that they would continue to target the company until the company agreed to stop targeting Local 2347.

The union followed up its successful Labour Day demonstration with a victory at the Niagara Falls Courtyard Marriott, when the hotel's room attendants, laundry workers, and gift shop staff voted in December 2008 to join Local 2347. "We really need to make things better at work and in the hotel industry as a whole in Niagara. I think that we can make a real difference for our families and for all tourism workers throughout the Niagara region," said Marie Oddson, a room attendant at the hotel and key union supporter.[59] Local 2347 was also busy organizing hotel workers in St. Catharines.

Early in 2009, Diane Barnim, a room attendant at the Holiday Inn on North Service Road in St. Catharines, became an overnight cause célèbre when Local 2347 featured her in a series of billboard ads aimed at rallying community support for workers' rights. Barnim, who had worked at the Holiday Inn for five years, was determined to improve working conditions at the hotel. In August 2008, she had contacted Local 2347 and, with the help of the union, had started signing up her co-workers on union cards in an effort to win union certification. A few days later, she was terminated. Arguing that hotel management fired Barnim because she was exercising her legal right to unionize, Local 2347 filed an unfair labour practice complaint against the Holiday Inn with the OLRB.[60]

In October, the OLRB ordered that Barnim be reinstated on an interim basis. A month later, workers at the hotel — twenty-five of whom had initially signed union cards — voted 35 to 1 against joining the union. The union complained that, by firing Barnim, hotel management had frightened the hotel staff, with the result that the outcome of vote was biased, and asked the OLRB to recognize Local 2347 as the bargaining agent for the workers even though the union had lost the certification vote. The union's position was founded on the premise that firing a key union supporter in the middle of a union drive has a chilling effect on the entire workforce, which would explain the striking discrepancy between the number of cards signed and the number of workers who actually cast ballots in favour of the union.[61]

Recognizing that legal processes often take a long time to come to a resolution, in February 2009 the union also launched a high-profile advertising campaign designed to apply pressure on both the Holiday Inn and the provincial government.[62] The "I Stand with Diane" campaign featured an interactive website, an online petition, and a series of billboards across the city featuring Barnim's picture and encouraging community members to "Stand with Diane." The union's campaign, which called on the provincial government to reinstate card-based union certification, attracted high-profile celebrity endorsements. Actors Sarah Polley and Danny Glover, musician Harry Belafonte, Welland MPP Peter Kormos, and Welland MP Malcolm Allen were all featured on the billboards along with Barnim.[63]

Actor Sarah Polley (*left*) poses with St. Catharines hotel worker Diane Barnim (*right*) as part of the "I Stand with Diane" campaign. Courtesy of UNITE HERE.

"What's happened is by firing Diane the employer has succeeded in totally poisoning the workplace," said Alex Dagg. "We've got a workplace filled with people who believe that if you join a union, you get fired. That's the message."[64] In less than two days, five hundred people from across North America had signed the union's online petition.[65] In April 2009, the owner of the hotel, facing both growing pressure as a result of the campaign and the very real prospect of having the OLRB side with the union, voluntarily recognized the union as the bargaining agent for the hotel's workers.

Local 2347's organizing victories and growing community presence forced employers like Canadian Niagara Hotels to rethink their relationship with the union. In April 2008, an arbitration decision had forced Canadian Niagara Hotels to make good on the unpaid wages that had become a central issue in the protests against the company. The decision vindicated the union's assertion that the company had not been abiding by the terms of the collective agreement. Local 2347 president Sandra Rebrovich trumpeted the arbitration award in a press release. "Hopefully soon," she commented, "this employer will figure out that it is easier to build a good working relationship with the members of our union than it is to play legal games."[66]

Someone at Canadian Niagara Hotels must have been listening. The union's intense and protracted battle to gain both recognition and cooperation from the company finally came to an end in January 2009, when members of Local 2347, now affiliated with Workers United, ratified a new contract. Both the union and management claimed that the deal would mark a positive turning point in labour relations between the parties. In a symbolic gesture of labour peace, the union decided to hold its 11–12 November 2010 Ontario Council meeting at the Brock Hotel (recently renamed the Crowne Plaza) — once a frequent target of union demonstrations. "I am so happy to have you all here in Niagara and inside this beautiful hotel rather than outside on the street!" Rebrovich declared in her opening address to union delegates.[67] The assembled activists erupted with loud applause and laughter before getting down to business. After all, there were still numerous outstanding challenges, opportunities, and obstacles facing working people seeking to improve working conditions in Niagara's hotel and hospitality sector.

# The House Advantage:
# Organizing Niagara's Casinos

Back in the early 1990s, city leaders in Niagara Falls, determined to pull the community out of an economic slump brought about by deindustrialization and a depressed tourism sector, asked the provincial government to allow the city to host a commercial casino and organized a referendum on the issue in conjunction with the November 1994 municipal elections. Casino proponents argued it would create jobs, attract investment, augment tax revenues, and correspondingly reduce the tax burden on local residents. Opponents of casino gambling feared an increase in crime and compulsive gambling, traffic congestion, and a heavier tax burden owing to a greater need for policing and other costs associated with the criminal justice system.[1]

Whereas opponents of casino gambling were based primarily in religious communities, the pro-casino forces included community leaders from all across the political spectrum, as well as representatives from both business and labour — including former CLC president Shirley Carr, who acted as co-chair of the YES campaign leading up to the referendum.[2] Carr's role was strategically important for the YES forces because it indicated that organized labour viewed casino gaming as an important source of jobs and, perhaps more importantly, as a key to the revitalization of Niagara's labour movement.

On election day, Niagara Falls voters decided that the advantages outweighed the disadvantages and endorsed casino gambling, with 63 percent casting ballots in favour of the referendum question. Just over two years later, Casino Niagara, nestled in the Clifton Hill tourist area, opened its doors to the public. From the very start, a number of labour unions showed active interest in organizing casino workers. However, despite multiple union drives by several different unions over the course of the past fifteen years, Niagara's casinos have, by and large, remained ununionized. The non-union status of the vast majority of casino workers in Niagara is somewhat surprising, given that most other casino workers across North America belong to labour unions and enjoy the higher wages and better working conditions typically associated with union membership. If the union advantage is so obvious, then why have Niagara's casino workers repeatedly rejected unionization?

Briefly put, casino management enjoys a "house advantage" in its efforts to avoid unionization. In the gaming industry, the house advantage refers to the profitable winning edge that the casino has over the player. Over the long term, the house advantage virtually guarantees the casino will always win. In the case of Niagara's casinos, management has perfected a union-avoidance strategy that relies on a complex mix of both union substitution and union suppression to dissuade casino workers from organizing.

When Casino Niagara opened its doors to the public in December 1996, HERE, the CAW, the Laborers' International Union of North America (LIUNA), the International Brotherhood of Teamsters, and the OPSEU all tested the waters. Casino workers complained about low wages, exposure to second-hand smoke, and preferential treatment for a privileged few. The various unions made their pitches to casino workers, and it soon became clear that the CAW had emerged as the favourite among pro-union employees. While the CAW's membership was based primarily in manufacturing, particularly in the automotive sector, it had a very good reputation as a strong union that was able to secure decent contracts for its members. The CAW had also recently organized workers at Casino Windsor, thus establishing an important toehold in Canada's emerging gaming industry.

After the CAW gathered enough support through card signing to trigger a certification election in early November 1999, CAW national president Buzz Hargrove made a personal visit to Casino Niagara. He chatted with casino workers about poor working conditions, air quality issues, and management's tendency to play favourites.[3] After a scrum with reporters outside the casino, Hargrove, armed with a roll of coins and a stack of chips, made his way inside. He was greeted by a security officer who asked for his autograph. Hargrove lost his money pretty quickly — it was a sign of things to come. Over a period of four days early in November 1999, the OLRB held a secret-ballot vote to determine the wishes of casino workers. In the end, the workers voted 1,169 to 1,064 against the CAW. The union blamed its narrow defeat in part on the provincial government's decision to do away with the card-based method of union certification, which had been used successfully in 1994 to organize casino workers in Windsor. In 1995, the Conservative government of Mike Harris replaced the card-based system with a mandatory vote system that had the effect of making it easier for employers to avoid unionization.

Under the old card-based system, in order to be recognized by the OLRB as the official bargaining agent for a group of workers, a union needed 55 percent of the employees in a workplace to sign union cards. In this system, the signatures collected on union cards represent a demonstration of the workers' desire to be represented by the union. Under the mandatory vote system, unions are required to sign up at least 40 percent of the employees on union cards, at which point the union can file a certification application with the OLRB. This application in turn triggers a mandatory vote five business days later, supervised by the board. The union is required to win at least 50 percent plus one of the votes cast in the secret-ballot certification election in order to become the official bargaining agent for the workers. During the five business days between the union's application and the certification vote, workers are typically bombarded with anti-union literature and an assortment of threats and promises from management designed to discourage workers from following through with unionization.[4] In effect, despite the vote by secret ballot, the system actually inhibits workplace democracy, providing employers with both the opportunity and the incentive to influence the outcome of the vote through intimidation, coercion, misinformation, or all of the above.[5]

In the wake of the CAW's unsuccessful bid for certification,

OPSEU announced that it would take a crack at unionizing Casino Niagara employees.[6] In February 2000, the union overcame casino management's house advantage by successfully organizing casino security guards, winning a certification election by a margin of 101 to 71 votes.[7] The union had hoped that this small victory would help to secure the support of casino workers in other departments, but the union's organizing drive eventually fizzled out, and the CAW returned to try a second time. By this time, however, casino management had perfected a very sophisticated union-avoidance strategy, consisting of two basic parts.

On the one hand, casino management has employed "union substitution" techniques that are designed to increase worker loyalty and thus make employees — or "associates," as casino management calls them — far less likely to identify with the interests of the union. These techniques have included signing bonuses, free dry cleaning services, educational reimbursements, casino-sponsored holiday parties and family picnics, and annual pay raises. Casino management has also tried to keep wages and working conditions more or less in line with those of unionized casino workers in Windsor. This has created a situation in which casino workers in Niagara receive comparable wages and vacation time provisions without having to pay union dues, which obviously undermines the incentive to unionize. In addition, casino management has provided mechanisms whereby employees can air their grievances and resolve disputes. These include open-door policies and formalized complaint procedures, which, although not legally enforceable, lend the impression that employee complaints are taken seriously and dealt with in a fair and consistent manner.

On the other hand, casino management has simultaneously pursued a strategy of union suppression, which is designed to plant seeds of doubt about unions in the minds of workers and play on worker fears concerning the impact of unionization on job security. The goal here is to cast the union as a self-interested and disruptive third party. Casino management's union suppression techniques have included the development of an anti-union website and frequent distribution of anti-union fact sheets, as well as captive-audience meetings intended to dissuade workers from unionizing.

Buzz Hargrove has argued that if workers are given the choice between having a union and not having a union, they will likely choose to have a union — but if workers are given a choice between having a union and having a job, they will always choose their job.[8] Hargrove's point is that casino management's union avoidance tactics have changed the nature of the certification vote itself, encouraging workers to vote on the basis of their fears rather than their hopes for the future.

Admittedly, some workers are genuinely uninterested in union membership, particularly those who earn a substantial portion of their income through tips. All the same, anti-union attitudes on the part of some workers cannot possibly explain why the CAW has repeatedly failed to organize Niagara's casinos. We know that support for unionization exists because workers are willing to sign union cards. And yet a significant number of workers who initially indicate support for the union ultimately vote against union representation in the secret-ballot certification election. This phenomenon was evident in March 2001, when the CAW narrowly lost its second certification vote — this time by a substantial margin of 1,701 to 820. Even though over 40 percent of the workers had signed union cards, less than a third of the workers ultimately voted in favour of CAW representation. Casino management's union-avoidance strategy was instrumental in dispelling much of the union support in the workplace. As CAW organizer Maureen Kirincic told local media, "Management put a lot of pressure on the workers and fought hard. Workers were given a 50 cents an hour raise just prior to the vote and they were led to believe they are going to get a bonus up to $1,000 and that whatever we bargained for Windsor they [management] would follow."[9] The strategy worked perfectly. A few months later, Casino Niagara initiated layoffs and scaled back hours for casino workers in all departments, prompting more than a few employees to second-guess their decision to reject the CAW.[10]

On 22 October 2001, construction began on a second casino, in the Fallsview area. The CAW knew that, once the new Fallsview Casino Resort opened its doors, it would be even more difficult to organize casino workers, given a much larger workforce spread across two different workplaces. For their part, Casino Niagara workers worried about what the opening of the new casino would mean for their jobs. Would Casino Niagara close down — and, if it did, would they be able to transfer to the new location? The uncertainty surrounding the opening of the Fallsview Casino Resort prompted renewed interest in union membership.[11] The CAW seized the opportunity to launch another organizing drive in advance of the opening of the new casino. It managed to sign the required number of workers on union cards, setting the stage for a certification vote in December 2003.

In response, casino management scheduled a series of paid captive-audience meetings with casino workers and provided them with thinly veiled anti-union literature to read before the vote. In a letter to casino management, CAW organizing director Paul Forder complained that the meetings constituted "nothing more than a direct attempt by you to bombard the workers with management views and opinions in an attempt to dissuade them from voting YES for the CAW. If you really respected your workers, you would not insult their intelligence by trying to tell them how to vote."[12] Casino management's campaign prevailed once again: Casino Niagara workers voted 1,334 to 907 against union representation. Dejected by a third straight defeat, the union went back to the drawing board.

A year later, another round of aggressive layoffs and shift reductions at the casinos sparked renewed interest in unionization. After scores of workers from both Casino Niagara and the Fallsview Casino Resort contacted the *Niagara Falls Review* to complain about the massive cutbacks, the newspaper penned an editorial chastising casino management. "So many people seem unhappy at the two casinos that the Canadian Auto Workers union may be met with open arms next time it tries to organize there," the paper warned.[13]

The next day, the CAW officially launched its fourth drive to unionize casino workers in Niagara Falls.

On 30 March 2005, in an effort to promote the union's organizing drive, fifty CAW retirees showed up at the Fallsview Casino Resort wearing bright green T-shirts featuring the CAW's logo and a message on the back: "Sign your CAW union card today." Once inside, the retirees scattered across the gaming floor, claiming seats at slot machines. The union's marketing ploy irked casino management, who instructed security guards to ask the retirees to either remove or change their T-shirts — prompting CAW retiree Dennis Hryorchuk to quip that visiting the casino nearly caused him to lose his shirt.[14] The incident attracted media attention and brought the union's organizing drive back into the spotlight. However, the union was having difficulty gathering the number of signed union cards required to trigger a vote, largely because of increased turnover in contract positions.

In November, the CAW announced it was creating a new local specifically for casino workers in Niagara. Local 21 — the number inspired by a natural blackjack — is just "good luck," explained CAW organizer Maureen Kirincic.[15] By creating a separate local, the CAW was addressing concerns among casino workers that their own workplace issues might be overshadowed by issues in the automotive sector — the union's traditional power base in Niagara. The union held a series of open houses for casino workers to field their questions and encourage them to sign union cards, but, in the end, the CAW could not muster enough support and was forced to put the organizing campaign on hold.[16]

Meanwhile, working conditions at Niagara's casinos went from bad to worse. In May 2007, members of Niagara Falls City Council started openly criticizing casino management's treatment of its workforce and of the community. Councillor Jim Diodati complained, "They're taking without giving. That seems to be the new philosophy."[17] Niagara Falls MPP Kim Craitor told the local media that he had similar concerns, adding, "I'm extremely frustrated by the way employees are treated down there."[18] However, the disappointment of local politicians did not convince the casinos to change their winning strategy for avoiding unionization.

In October 2007, amid rumours that the provincial government was considering closing Casino Niagara, the CAW partnered with Local 2347 of the hotel workers' union to launch an online petition campaign in support of hospitality workers in Niagara. The text of the petition reflected a prevailing sense in the community of the gap between the casinos' promise of year-round well-paying jobs for all tourism workers in Niagara and the reality of economic life for those same workers.

> We the undersigned believe the following: Having two casinos in Niagara Falls is vital to the continued economic prosperity of the city.
>
> Prosperity will only be guaranteed if the jobs at the casino and in the surrounding tourism industry are good jobs.
>
> Goods jobs are jobs where: workers earn a living wage that allows them to support their families in dignity, workers are respected and receive the training they require to work safely and pursue career advancement opportunities, workers are ensured of benefits, including secure pensions, workers are free to join and be active in unions where their collective bargaining rights are respected.
>
> So as to advance the interests of everyone in Niagara Falls, workers must be included in discussions surrounding the future of the casinos. Workers must be given the opportunity to select representatives who will be at the table alongside the hotel owners and other interested parties.
>
> Background: Niagara Falls' two casinos are an important part of our local economy and employ more people than the city's next 8 largest employers combined. Those other 8 employers are hotel and restaurant companies which are at least partially dependent on the casino to attract visitors to Niagara Falls.
>
> Fifty years ago, things looked very different in the Niagara region. While there was a thriving tourism industry, the bulk of

our local economy was centred on manufacturing and the jobs it created in our community. The loss of those manufacturing jobs has directly affected the standard of living for people in Niagara. While the 1960s saw our region enjoying one of the highest per capita incomes in Canada, the Niagara region now has the lowest median income in all of Ontario.

Families in Niagara Falls are struggling. Many workers in this area are making very close to the minimum wage and are subject to seasonal unemployment as is typical in the tourism industry. And yet the tourism industry in Niagara Falls continues to reap massive profits each year.

If we want Niagara Falls and all of its citizens to prosper, we need to demand more than just the simple fact that our two casinos remain open. We also need to demand that the jobs at those two casinos and in the surrounding tourism industry are the kind of good jobs that can sustain our families and allow us to live in security and dignity. We need to ensure the people who work at the casinos and the surrounding hotels are just as involved in discussions between the city and the province on the casinos' future as the tourism owners clearly already are.

Workers are prepared to get involved if they are only given the chance.[19]

Soon after the provincial government laid to rest rumours that Casino Niagara might close its doors, the CAW, UNITE HERE, and LIUNA all initiated campaigns to organize casino workers. However, the latter two unions did not manage to make much headway, and once again the CAW emerged as the most promising option for pro-union casino workers.

The CAW hammered away at the issue of job security in its communications to casino workers. According to figures released by the union, 84.5 percent of casino workers held full-time positions in 2003. By 2009, that number had dropped to just 57 percent.[20] The CAW also argued that the percentage of temporary workers had jumped from 3.5 percent in 2003 to 17 percent in 2009.[21] In effect, for a growing proportion of casino workers, casino management had turned what were supposed to be steady full-time jobs into part-time, casual work. This served casino management's union-avoidance strategy perfectly. Contract employees were less likely to support unionization owing to the precarious nature of their employment and fears that unionization would lead to the elimination of contract positions.

In January 2010, the CAW filed an application for certification, which it later withdrew when it discovered that hundreds of occasional banquet servers had been unaccounted for in its calculations.[22] The CAW would need more signed union cards in order to meet the 40 percent threshold needed to trigger a certification election under the Labour Relations Act. In the weeks that followed, the union continued to promote the issue of job security in an effort to gather the additional cards it needed. At a meeting of the CAW Gaming Council in Niagara Falls in March 2010, longtime Casino Niagara employee Romel Argueta reinforced the union's job security message in a speech he delivered about the state of the gaming industry in Niagara:

> I started working for Casino Niagara in 1996, almost 14 years now. I remember very well the opening day of Casino Niagara. Everybody in this community — local politicians, small business, our families, in particular, we, the ones who got a job at Casino Niagara. We were so pleased to have the opportunity to bring these full-time jobs to our communities.
>
> Back then, the majority got a full-time job. That's not the case today. That's not the case these days. These casinos are no longer providing full-time jobs in our communities. Instead, seasonal work, contracts, part-time jobs are increasing. We, the workers in these communities, we need to provide our children a good education, health care, shelter, food, clothing, etc. In order to do that, we need full-time. . . . We have the second highest unemployment rate in the country. One in every six children in our communities lives in poverty.

We're not going to reduce poverty, inequality with these precarious jobs. I think these days more than ever, we — the workers in these communities — we need unions. But also, we need progressive, local politicians. And together we can stand up to these corporations, to these multi-million corporations, and say enough is enough — we are not going to allow you to come here and disrespect our workers in our communities. That's what we need to do.[23]

Soon afterwards, the CAW was able to submit its application to the OLRB, triggering a certification election in April 2010.

While the CAW was busy convincing workers to support the union, casino management was walking a thin legal line in its communications to workers prior to the certification election. For example, employers are not allowed to tell workers that unionization will result in a workplace closure. However, casino management provided workers with data showing that workplaces organized by the CAW (mostly in the manufacturing sector) had experienced thousands of layoffs and job losses over the course of the previous few years.[24] Management also told workers that unionization would mean building a new employment contract from scratch — creating the impression that a collective agreement negotiated by the union might leave them worse off in terms of wages, benefits, and working conditions.[25] Casino management went even further on the issue of job security, arguing "the union cannot guarantee your job secuity — however, your membership helps guarantee the union's job security."[26] This type of employer communication, which portrays the union as a self-interested third party, is common in union-avoidance campaigns, as it reinforces the idea that workers have more in common with their employers than they do with any union. This anti-union strategy also frames the certification decision as a risky gamble for workers, in the hope that employees will remain loyal to the employer even in the face of poor working conditions.

Casino management also exploited worker fears about the prospect of strikes and lockouts. Despite the fact that 97 percent of all

CAW negotiations are concluded without a strike, in a communication to workers in advance of the certification election, casino management wrote: "We're not saying unionization will lead to a strike, but every CAW-represented Casino worksite has been on strike."[27] Although the union repeatedly attempted to quell workers' fears concerning the assertions and innuendo proffered by casino management, their efforts were not entirely successful.

On the first day of the April 2010 union certification vote at the two casinos, the *Niagara Falls Review* published letters from both CAW president Ken Lewenza and Art Frank, president of Niagara Casinos, which encapsulated their respective positions on unionization.

### Ken Lewenza, Canadian Autoworkers Union

There's no question that for thousands of Niagara casino workers this week's union certification vote has been a long time coming.

Since the casinos opened their doors, workers have expressed a willingness to speak for themselves at work, with a collective voice equal with their employer. This is the basis for true workplace democracy.

Sure, my teeth were cut on the auto assembly line. But I can tell you, there aren't a lot of folks tougher than those who have put in their time on the casino floor. Dealing with the public on a daily basis, whether it's working the floor, serving cocktails or slogging away in back rooms, these workers have generated billions in profits for their employer and their province with no fair value in return.

Casino workers are a major force in Canada's tourism industry and play an important role in generating the wealth that contributes to our social and economic development. Even in the worst economic downturn in recent history, Ontario's gaming workers still helped rake in hundreds of millions in third quarter revenue for the O.L.G. in 2009.

Nearly half of that was generated by Niagara's casinos.

Yet the hourly earnings of most gaming workers (similar to

most non-union service sector workers in the gaming sector and elsewhere) still lie well below Canada's industrial average. Worse still, their work hours are sporadic and simply out of their control.

Many have been led to believe that full-time work, or at the very least guaranteed part-time work hours, is a luxury. They have come to think it selfish or inappropriate to demand good workplace benefits.

How do I know this? As president of C.A.W. Local 444 in Windsor, I stood with thousands of casino workers in their heroic and historic drive to organize, demanding respect and a quality of work life from their employer. I felt their frustrations and I listened to their concerns.

That organizing drive, and the subsequent collective agreements we were able to negotiate, changed the face of collective bargaining in the Canadian gaming sector. It was an emotional and inspiring victory.

Today, C.A.W. represents more than 7,000 casinos, slots and racetrack workers in Canada, making us the country's largest gaming sector union.

Despite what many observers may think, joining a union isn't about being spiteful towards an employer, and it's certainly not about damaging business (what jobs would be left if that were the case?). For casino workers, it's always been a question of respect and fairness at work.

Antagonism, hostility and public resentment are often bred when employers choose to ignore those rights and, instead, spend untold amounts of time and energy trying to convince workers that they have their best interests at heart. In this employer's case, it's been 14 years' worth.

Casino workers will head to the voting booth this week, with the full support of C.A.W. members across the country, demanding fairness, equality and a true sense of empowerment from their boss — once and for all.

No worker should demand less.

### Art Frank, President of Niagara Casinos

Since 1998, the C.A.W. has attempted unsuccessfully to become the trade union representing the associates at Niagara Casinos on four separate occasions.

The fifth such attempt will take place Wednesday, Thursday and Friday at polling stations at Fallsview Casino and as an organization, we have always maintained we prefer to deal directly with our associates rather than through a third-party like the C.A.W.

Over the past 13 years, we have demonstrated we are an employer of choice in the Niagara region thanks to an excellent compensation and benefits package — the best in Niagara and the best among all other commercial casino operations in Ontario.

Niagara Casinos has a corporate culture that allows associates to work in a safe environment of dignity and respect in which they are not only free — but encouraged — to bring any employment issues to our attention.

Since joining the Niagara Casinos team, I have said that the only thing that guarantees job security is a viable business. We have persevered despite countless challenges and today we have a viable business.

Our associates are faced with an extremely important decision — a decision that should not be left for others to make on their behalf.

We recognize the ability of our associates to make informed decisions in matters relating to their employment and we will always respect those decisions.

I encourage all associates of Niagara Casinos to take the time to vote; today from 4 to 8 p.m. and 10 p.m. to 1 a.m., or Thursday and Friday 8 to 10 a.m., 4 to 8 p.m. and 10 p.m. to 1 a.m. Polls will be open at these times at both Fallsview Casino and Casino Niagara in the associate dining rooms.

This is a vote for you and your family and your working relationship at Niagara Casinos.

Your vote counts. Your vote matters.[28]

The CAW spent the next few days calling members who signed union cards reminding them to vote and offered rides to their supporters in order to ensure maximum turnout.[29] For its part, casino management offered to cover taxi fare to get workers to the polling station and offered financial incentives to workers from out of town who showed up to vote outside of their regularly scheduled shifts.[30] In the end, casino workers rejected unionization once again, this time by a vote of 1,806 to 1,047.

CAW organizer John Aman tried to find a silver lining in the result. He told the local media, "Our solid support is increasing. Clearly, it's a wake-up call for the company on many aspects. All is not lost."[31] Casino management was pleased with the result. Company spokesperson Greg Medulun did acknowledge that "a number of our associates believe representation is required," adding that "we consider this an opportunity to explore a potential change to our workplace environment."[32] However, Medulun also heaped praise on the casino's management team. Before the ballots were counted, he told the *Niagara Falls Review* that "from the moment we were given notice C.A.W. was attempting to certify our associates, the management team worked to ensure [they] had the opportunity to educate themselves."[33] But what kind of education did casino management deliver to its workforce? Did workers confidently cast ballots armed with all the information they needed, or did they fall victim to casino management's union-avoidance strategy?

The CAW continues to argue that casino management's use of union substitution and union suppression tactics, combined with the provincial government's refusal to reinstate card-based union certification, have solidified casino management's house advantage in combatting unionization.[34] This dismal assessment, however, has not prevented the union from fighting against the odds. Niagara's casino workers are still plagued by a lack of job security in an economic and political climate threatened by currency fluctuations, cross-border delays, and high energy prices. Labour unions potentially hold the key to a better, more certain, future for these workers.

But as the case of Niagara's casinos has demonstrated, unionization is highly contested, and employers are willing to fight tooth and nail to avoid having to deal with unions. All the same, the CAW persists in active efforts to organize casino workers in Niagara.

# Migrant Farm Workers in Niagara

Agricultural workers in Niagara have faced greater obstacles to gaining union power than any other group of workers, largely because the law excludes them from many of the labour rights available to the rest of the workforce in Canada.

As far back as the beginning of the twentieth century, Niagara farmers had to import immigrant women from Buffalo during the harvest season to pick fruits and vegetables. Because the work was physically demanding, ill-paid, and temporary, it was generally avoided by workers who had other options. Growers were thus forced to rely on marginalized groups of workers. During the inter-war years, the consolidation of canners and food retailers intensified pressure on growers to sell their produce at lower prices. The growers could maintain profitability only by paying seasonal workers low wages.[1] During this time, immigrant women, whose number in Niagara increased after World War I, provided the bulk of seasonal agricultural labour in the area. Understandably, however, they gravitated toward more permanent or better-paid jobs whenever such jobs became available. Consequently, during the Second World War, when many immigrant women found manufacturing jobs thanks to the enlistment of men and the growth in war production, farmers were forced to find new sources of labour. Japanese Canadians forcibly relocated from coastal British Columbia and excluded from most other types of work as a result of racism and discrimination picked, packed, and canned fruits and vegetables in the region.[2] Their ranks were augmented by high school students brought to Niagara during the agricultural season by government programs. Since the students generally returned to school in September, and because hiring and housing them required special provisions, their employment was strictly a wartime emergency measure.

After the war, the government once again stepped in, offering contracts to refugees and immigrants from war-torn Europe, who would work for a year for specific employers in agriculture and other sectors suffering from labour shortages, as a condition for gaining entry to Canada. This denial of labour mobility — a key right for Canadian citizens — was the only way to guarantee the availability of workers to tend and harvest highly perishable fruits and field crops in Niagara. Once they fulfilled their contracts, however, these workers also left the agricultural sector in search of more secure, better-paid work.[3]

In the 1960s, state officials tried to fill seasonal agricultural jobs in Niagara and elsewhere in southern Ontario with Native workers from northern Ontario reserves. But while the officials saw migration to agricultural jobs in the south as a way of encouraging Native people to assimilate into mainstream society, many Native workers preferred to return to their reserves at the end of the harvest season.[4]

In 1966, the federal government launched the Seasonal Agricultural Workers Program (SAWP), a migrant worker program designed to address the enduring problem of labour shortages in the agricultural industry. The program, which still exists, brings Caribbean and Mexican workers to Canada on a seasonal basis to work on farms and in greenhouses. It has in fact expanded dramatically over the past few decades, as employers in the agricultural sector have become ever more reliant on migrant labour.[5] Indeed, because the growth of temporary worker programs coincided with deindustrialization and hence with the decline of immigration to Niagara, migrant workers with no right to obtain permanent resident status are now more visible than immigrants in the region.

Thousands of migrant agricultural workers arrive in Niagara each year to work on farms, in orchards, and, increasingly, in nurseries and greenhouses. The vast majority of these labourers are married men, from Mexico or Jamaica, who leave their families behind for most of the year in hopes of providing them with a better life back home. Most make slightly more than minimum wage. While popular with employers, the SAWP has been criticized by labour activists and others who argue that the program institutionalizes exploitation.

In September 2008, the St. Catharines and District Labour Council and the Centre for Labour Studies at Brock University co-sponsored a film screening and panel discussion on migrant agricultural labour in Niagara. The event began with a screening of the award-winning National Film Board documentary *El Contrato*. The documentary, which explores the appalling living and working conditions of migrant agricultural labour in Leamington, Ontario, takes direct aim at the federal government's SAWP. In one of the film's most poignant scenes, a worker from Mexico, who complains about employer abuse and exploitation, tells the filmmaker, "In my mind, slavery has not yet disappeared." [6]

After the screening, Min Sook Lee, the film's director, joined a representative from the United Food and Commercial Workers and local migrant agricultural workers in a panel discussion of the challenges facing the growing ranks of migrant agricultural workers in Niagara. With the help of a translator, the workers took turns describing feelings of isolation and exploitation and testifying to poor housing conditions, difficult working conditions, and employers who care more about the bottom line than the health and safety of workers. The timing of the event was significant in that it coincided with the Niagara Wine Festival — one of the region's premier events. Although the grape and wine industry is integral to the region's economy and cultural identity, the migrant agricultural workers who sustain the industry are completely excluded from the festival. Showcasing the actual process of wine production would require telling the stories of hundreds of migrant agricultural workers and their struggles with isolation and substandard working conditions — a reality that would not mesh well with the Wine Festival's elite image of swank decadence. Given that the festival is an important source of advertising revenue, it is hardly surprising that local media chose not to cover the panel discussion.

Even though the plight of migrant agricultural workers in Niagara has garnered little media attention, unions, church-based groups, and community organizations have made a concerted effort to raise the profile and dignity of offshore workers by organizing social events and acting as advocates for improved training, housing, and occupational safety.[7]

Back in October 1994, the United Food and Commercial Workers Union, spurred by a complaint received from a Jamaican agricultural worker in Niagara, held a press conference to shed light on the deplorable treatment of migrant workers in Ontario. Walter Lumsden, president of UFCW Local 1993, and Ralph Ortlieb, regional director of the Service Employees International Union, explained that they had been able to gain a very direct and personal understanding of the conditions under which migrant agricultural labourers work and live by touring several local farms dressed as farm workers. Lumsden and Ortlieb indicated that their findings confirmed what they had heard from migrant workers during a secret meeting organized by the union in an abandoned Niagara-on-the-Lake farmhouse.[8] "We found everything, from workers being sent into fields just hours after the crop had been sprayed to workers with sores all over their bodies," Lumsden told the press conference.[9] In terms of housing, the union leaders described the situation as "beyond description," explaining that migrant workers are often forced to live in sheds or trailers, without any utilities. The union estimated that mistreatment of migrant agricultural workers was widespread and that any attempt by workers to assert their rights was met by threats and intimidation by farm employers.[10]

For their part, local farmers dismissed the union's claims as sensational. In the ensuing years, however, more and more worker and community organizations began to echo the concerns of the

UFCW about the plight of migrant agricultural workers not only in Niagara but all across Canada. Petra Kukacka, president of ENLACE Community Link, a Mexican migrant worker support organization, described the situation as follows:

> The interests of the governments involved defer to the interests of farmers and the profit margin, which often means long hours, little pay and few benefits for the workers. Although many workers are thankful for the opportunity to work, reciting accounts of positive experiences and expressing excitement about not being idle, there are many whose experiences include abuse and exploitation on a daily basis. For these workers, the S.A.W.P. does not present as an opportunity to convert their skills and hard work into purchasing power back home; it is seen more as a jail sentence where his or her only "crime" is that of being a citizen of a developing country struggling for a grip on globalization's spoils. Absent from the S.A.W.P. is any viable mechanism which might work effectively to put an end to experiences of exploitation and abuse. In the end, workers are beholden to the goodwill of their employer which, too often, is not forthcoming.[11]

Vincenzo Pietropaolo, a photographer and journalist who has documented the lives of migrant workers in Canada, makes a similar argument. According to Pietropaolo, "the principle of being 'beholden' to your employer for all your needs, even after work, is reminiscent of the indentured labour practices of the nineteenth century, whereby immigrants came to North America on contract to work for a number of years in exchange for passage and accommodation. Although the practice is different today, the principle of near-total dependence on the goodwill of the employer is not."[12] Pietropaolo's eloquent photograph of migrant farm workers being driven into the city of St. Catharines by their employer after work simply reinforces his provocative argument

Migrant workers being transported into St. Catharines.
Courtesy of Vincenzo Pietropaolo.

In response to concerns about worker loneliness and isolation, faith communities in rural Niagara launched the Caribbean Workers Outreach Program, which aims to address the spiritual needs of migrant workers and involve them in social activities outside the farms. Growing Respect for Offshore Workers (GROW), a community organization dedicated to building relationships with migrant farm labour in Niagara-on-the-Lake, established the "Migrant Worker Fan Club," which provides workers with electric fans in the summer months in order to make life more bearable in their poorly ventilated living quarters.[13] In 2004, the UFCW, in partnership with the Agriculture Workers Alliance (AWA), established an agricultural worker support centre in the village of Virgil. The centre offers free support and advocacy services, helping temporary foreign agricultural workers with health insurance claims, parental leave benefits, and workers' compensation.[14] Also available through the centre are English as a second language classes and workshops on everything from occupational health and safety to bicycle safety. The centre has become an important resource for migrant agricultural labourers in the Niagara region.

The AWA has been at the forefront of calls to reform the federal government's Seasonal Agricultural Workers Program so as to ensure stronger protection for temporary agricultural workers, including full collective bargaining rights, as well as a path to landed immigrant status.[15] Since the AWA set up shop in Virgil, the wages and living conditions of migrant agricultural workers have steadily improved. The existence of the AWA and other watchdog groups has effectively put pressure on farmers to increase wages and to treat workers in a more humane fashion. However, migrant agricultural workers continue to be excluded, by law, from accessing many of the labour rights available to Canadians working in other industries.[16]

In 2003, the UFCW launched three legal challenges in support of migrant agricultural labour. The first, *Fraser v. Ontario (Attorney General)*, challenged the constitutional validity of the provincial government's Agricultural Employees Protection Act, which granted agricultural workers the freedom to "associate" but, absurdly, not the related rights to strike or to bargain collectively. The second challenged the exclusion of agricultural workers from the province's Occupational Health and Safety Act. The third asked the courts to strike down a law requiring mandatory Employment Insurance deductions for seasonal foreign workers, on the grounds that these workers are not eligible to collect Employment Insurance benefits.[17]

When the federal government argued that the union could not legitimately represent migrant agricultural workers who were not members of the UFCW, the legal challenge concerning access to Employment Insurance was derailed. Instead, the union capitalized on a decision by the Employment Insurance Board of Referees to extend parental benefits to SAWP workers by antedating thousands of cases, thereby winning millions of dollars' worth of benefits for migrant workers.[18] In 2006, the UFCW also succeeded in gaining health and safety coverage for agricultural workers from the provincial government. In April 2011, the Supreme Court of Canada finally rendered a decision in the *Fraser* case, ruling that Ontario's

Agricultural Employees Protection Act did not violate the guarantee of freedom of association found in section 2d of the Charter of Rights and Freedoms.[19] The UFCW's heavy reliance on expensive and time-consuming legal strategies to protect and enhance workers' rights has thus produced mixed results. More importantly, though, these results underscore the extent to which politicians and legislatures have been unwilling to help drive organized labour's agenda forward.

In view of this situation, some migrant workers and their allies have turned to direct action to influence public opinion. On 4 September 2011, roughly sixty migrant agricultural workers and dozens of their allies descended on the Niagara region as part of the "migrant worker solidarity caravan." [20] The event, organized by Justicia for Migrant Workers, brought together migrant agricultural workers from Mexico, Jamaica, the Barbados, Trinidad and Tobago, Guatemala, and Thailand to highlight the plight of migrant labourers working in Niagara's multi-billion dollar agricultural industry and to demand improvements to Canada's labour laws. Organizers chose the Salem Chapel First British Methodist Episcopal Church on Geneva Street in St. Catharines as the departure point for the caravan. The choice was historically significant: the Geneva Street church had been a key stop on the Underground Railroad, the secret and informal network of routes and safe houses set up by abolitionists and used by black slaves in the United States to escape to Canada in the 1850s.[21] Tzazna Miranda Leal, an organizer with Justicia for Migrant Workers, explained the significance of launching the caravan from this particular spot:

We are here to pay homage to the struggles of the past, and the tremendous sacrifices undertaken by those who travelled along the Underground Railroad. Freedom was the dream that brought them north, yet today Canada's temporary foreign workers are subjected to conditions that deny migrants rights to fair treatment. We demand an end to indentureship.[22]

From St. Catharines, the caravan made its way to Virgil and on to Niagara-on-the-Lake, where migrant workers passed out peaches to bemused tourists in the Old Town. The workers also distributed brochures to passers-by explaining the purpose of their caravan and reminded restaurant patrons in the quaint dining establishments along Queen Street to thank a migrant worker for their meals. All along, the workers waved placards reading, "Justice, Respect, and Dignity" and "We Demand Better Medical Care." They also encouraged the public to think about the part played by towns in the Niagara region in the Underground Railroad and to ask themselves, "Do these towns still symbolize freedom and hope or do they now evoke oppression and exploitation?"[23] Caravan organizer Chris Ramsaroop explained to local media that workers were taking a "tremendous risk" by joining the caravan because it would make them vulnerable to possible retribution by their employers and perhaps even to deportation.[24] Nonetheless, the migrant workers clearly saw participation in the Labour Day weekend caravan as a risk worth taking in pursuit of justice, dignity, and respect in both their workplaces and their host communities.

# Organized Labour and the New Democratic Party in Niagara

On 1 June 1960, the St. Catharines and District Labour Council adopted a resolution endorsing the CLC's drive to create a new political party in Canada that would represent working-class interests first and foremost. The Labour Council was an enthusiastic supporter of the New Party. Only one delegate to the council voted against the resolution — Gerry Haugerud, of Local 268 of the IAM, who told delegates, "My local doesn't feel it should tell its members how to vote."[1] Labour Council president John Ideson scoffed at this suggestion, arguing instead that "organized labor is losing more members through unemployment, automation, plant shutdowns and senseless government policies than it will ever lose through taking political action."[2]

The council made a contribution to the New Party Founding Fund and worked energetically to build NDP riding associations after the party's founding convention in 1961. Although the labour-NDP alliance did not produce immediate results for workers in Niagara, the overlap between union leadership and NDP leadership was strong.

On 18 September 1975, Mel Swart made history by becoming the first NDP candidate from Niagara to win election to the Ontario legislature. As the new MPP for the Welland riding, Swart championed the cause of organized labour at Queen's Park. Swart inherited his democratic socialist values from his father, an organizer for the CCF during the Great Depression. Raised a Methodist, Swart believed in the social gospel and dedicated his life to ensuring that wealth was distributed more equitably.[3] His first successful bid for election took place in 1948 when he won a spot on Thorold Township Council. Swart served for eighteen years on council — the last eleven of those years as reeve. He later moved into regional politics and was elected as Thorold's representative to the Niagara Regional Council. While serving on Thorold Township Council, Swart ran for the CCF in a 1950 by-election, and then again in 1953, 1957, and 1958, finishing third in each contest. After the CCF became the NDP, Swart once again ran for the party in the 1962 federal election. He lost, at which point he switched to provincial politics. He finished second to the Conservative incumbent in both the 1967 and 1971 elections before finally winning the Welland riding in the 1975 provincial election. Swart went on to win re-election easily in 1977, 1981, 1985, and 1987. Aside from his political career, Swart was an active member of his church, served on the Brock University Founders Committee, and volunteered for countless community groups.[4] His multiple defeats before his historic election victory have long served as a reminder to Niagara New Democrats that election wins do not come easily but that the right combination of hard work, perseverance, and determination will eventually pay off. Higher levels of union density and a particular mix of supportive ethnic groups in the Welland riding also helped to boost NDP fortunes there relative to surrounding Niagara ridings, making it the most fertile terrain for left-wing politics in the region.

Niagara-area labour council presidents present Mel Swart with an award for his contribution to the local labour movement. Courtesy of the St. Catharines and District Labour Council.

Swart's election, combined with an economic and political shift to the right over the course of the late 1970s, marked the end of any significant communist influence on the local labour movement and its politics. This was confirmed in 1980, when a slate of social democrats led by Len Harrison of UAW Local 199 took over the St. Catharines and District Labour Council, thus solidifying the labour-NDP alliance.[5] Throughout the early 1980s, the labour-NDP partnership was stronger than ever at both the national and local levels. CAW Local 199 president and St. Catharines and District Labour Council vice president Garry Michaud ran for the party in the 1984 federal election and placed second in the St. Catharines riding, capturing roughly 30 percent of the popular vote. The NDP also placed second in the Niagara Falls riding. The party had momentum in Niagara.

After his retirement in 1988, Swart, the lone NDP representative in Niagara, passed the torch to Peter Kormos, a criminal defence lawyer and Welland city councillor, who overcame a smear campaign to win a by-election in the riding of Welland-Thorold in 1988. Two years later, Kormos was joined by four more NDP MPPs from Niagara as part of Ontario's first NDP government. Kormos was easily re-elected in September 1990, winning more than 60 percent of the popular vote. He served as minister of Consumer and Commercial Relations and minister of Financial Institutions, until Bob Rae removed him from cabinet for his reputation as a maverick and his refusal to compromise on the party's campaign commitment to implement a system of public automobile insurance.[6]

Christel Haeck, elected in the riding of St. Catharines-Brock, was a librarian, a local CUPE president, and a member of the executive of the St. Catharines and District Labour Council. She served as the parliamentary assistant to the minister of Colleges and Universities. Margaret Harrington, elected in the riding of Niagara Falls, was a member of Niagara Falls City Council, a local high school teacher, and a committed feminist. She served as parliamentary assistant to the minister of Housing and later as deputy speaker. Shirley Coppen, elected in the riding of Niagara South, was a registered nursing assistant and president of the Welland and District Labour Council. Coppen served as chief government whip, minister without portfolio, and later as minister of Labour in the provincial cabinet. Ron Hansen, elected in the riding of Lincoln, was a maintenance engineer at GM who sat on the government back benches. The fact that there were three successful female candidates from Niagara demonstrated how far women had come in the political realm since winning the franchise in 1918.

The recession of the early 1990s was, for Ontario, the worst economic downturn since the Great Depression. Niagara's manufacturing base was hit particularly hard owing to high interest rates, a strong Canadian dollar, and the impact of the Canada-US free trade agreement. At the ballot box, the Ontario NDP benefitted from the economic insecurity that workers and their families were experiencing. Voters moved to the NDP in droves, in hopes that the party would not fight the recession on the backs of the working class. However, once elected to office, Bob Rae's NDP government found it difficult to manage its long-standing relationship with organized labour, particularly in the face of a severe economic recession.[7]

The Ontario NDP's record in office has been the subject of much debate. A deep recession, hostility on the part of the media, a suspicious senior civil service, and political inexperience have all been blamed for the party's poor performance as a government.[8] One thing is clear, however: Bob Rae's government forever changed the relationship between organized labour and the NDP.

The former Liberal government of David Peterson left the newly elected Rae government with a hefty budget deficit, and Ontario's looming recession would only make the province's financial situation worse.[9] Fighting Ontario's devastating recession was rapidly driving up the province's debt. In response, the Rae government introduced an austerity program known as the Social Contract, which reopened collective agreements in the public sector and rolled back the wages of public sector union members by means of mandatory unpaid days off, known as "Rae Days." The government argued that its plan to reduce its wage bill by $2 billion through the Social Contract would allow it to preserve jobs while also controlling the deficit. However, union leaders argued that the Social Contract was an attack on basic trade union freedoms.[10]

In early June 1993, roughly one hundred CUPE members picketed the office of St. Catharines-Brock NDP MPP Christel Haeck. Touting the government's line, Haeck called the Social Contract "ground-breaking legislation in how to restructure government and the employee-employer relationship."[11] But her former union colleagues did not share her view. Brian McCormick, president of the Niagara District CUPE Council, lamented, "I worked to help elect a government that would be an ear for us. This is very disheartening."[12] Others were less reserved. "I'm ashamed of my party, the New Democratic Party," proclaimed CUPE Ontario President Sid

Ryan.[13] Haeck shook off the criticism. "I understand the rhetoric and concern of unions," she said. "I'd be doing the same thing. But to avoid significant job losses, they have to get a settlement."[14]

The Social Contract had a profoundly negative impact on the Rae government's relationship with organized labour and precipitated an exodus of rank-and-file union members from the party. The Social Contract also pitted unions who were loyal to the NDP against unions who were directly affected by the government's austerity program. The disunity of the labour movement during this period made it extremely difficult for unions to tackle important political issues in a concerted and effective manner.

At the local level, Haeck's unwavering support for the Social Contract drove a wedge between the NDP and the St. Catharines and District Labour Council. Haeck appeared before her former colleagues at the Labour Council to explain the government's position, but she did not find many sympathetic delegates. After a fractious debate, the Labour Council decided not to endorse Haeck's re-election bid.[15] Niagara South MPP Shirley Coppen was similarly rebuffed by her former union allies at election time.

On 14 June 1993, St. Catharines native Karen Haslam, NDP MPP for the riding of Perth and minister without portfolio in the Rae government, resigned from the cabinet over her opposition to the Social Contract.[16] She later joined Welland-Thorold NDP MPP Peter Kormos and one other NDP caucus member in voting against the legislation at Queen's Park. Kormos explained his opposition to the Social Contract in an article for the 1993 St. Catharines and District Labour Council *Labour Review,* which featured a cover with the acronym "NDP" going up in flames.

In little more than 90 days after the proposition of a social contract was presented to the N.D.P. Caucus at Queen's Landing in Niagara-on-the-Lake, Bill 48 became law. Only three members of the N.D.P. Caucus voted "no." I was proud to be among the three.

As a longtime New Democrat, I am far from proud of this government's record with working people. Bill 48, Bob Rae's "Social

Contract," is but the culmination of a series of significant reversals of longtime N.D.P. policies. I believe firmly that to call it a "betrayal" is mild. I believe strongly in the rights of workers to collectively bargain and to do so freely without fear that there will be interference with the negotiated results. Social contract legislation will directly attack free collective bargaining and turn contracts into meaningless pieces of paper. Who would have thought that it would be an N.D.P. government that would legislatively nullify collective bargaining agreements?

Some M.P.P.s voted for Bill 48 believing it was the right thing to do and an adequate response (for reasons beyond me) to the fiscal and economic crises. There were far more people in the government caucus who had great reservations about Bill 48 and noted its many flaws. Those from trade union backgrounds found it repugnant. Sadly, they voted for the Social Contract legislation. They'll have to answer to the people of Ontario.

I believed in September 1990 that this new government would do great things in the province of Ontario. It could show Ontario and the rest of Canada that government could be different. This has not been the case. I understand the right of the Premier as leader of the party to try to take the party in new directions. At the same time, as a member of the party I have a right to resist that direction if I feel it is wrong. Too many people worked too hard to see the C.C.F. [and] then the N.D.P., as a voice for working women and men, flourish for one person to destroy it. The growing cynicism about governments has only been heightened by the passage of Bill 48. It is but the culmination of a series of betrayals of longtime N.D.P. policy. First, the abandonment of public auto insurance and the abandonment of justice for innocent accident victims, then the complete reversal on a common pause day for retail workers and for communities and now an out-and-out attack on free collective bargaining.

I encourage working people to fight back, to let this government know that an economic war measures act is not the answer to our province's economic difficulties. Let the government know that all of us expect far more from our politicians and our political leaders. Years of Tory ideology, cutbacks and slashes in Ottawa was bad enough. We don't need it coming from Queen's Park.[17]

The 1993 federal election, which took place a few months after passage of the Social Contract Act, saw the defeat of every single federal NDP MP in Ontario. In Niagara, NDP candidates won, on average, an embarrassing 5 percent of the popular vote. On 22 November 1993, the OFL passed a resolution condemning those NDP MPPs who had voted for the Social Contract Act.[18] Among the delegates supporting the resolution was Ontario NDP president Julie Davis. "It's sad we've come to this," she lamented.[19] Without the support of the labour movement, the NDP's future seemed uncertain at best. In June 1995, most NDP candidates across Ontario suffered devastating defeats in the provincial election. In Niagara, Peter Kormos managed to hold on to his Welland-Thorold seat, largely because of his personal popularity and principled opposition to some of his own government's policies. In St. Catharines, St. Catharines-Brock, Niagara Falls, Lincoln, and Niagara South, NDP candidates suffered from a lack of volunteers and union resources, and all finished a distant third. The Mike Harris Conservatives swept into power with an explicitly pro-corporate and anti-union agenda, leaving many union activists wondering whether abandoning the NDP had only made a bad situation worse.

However, the silver lining for activists in the labour movement was that the weakening of the labour-NDP partnership led to unprecedented grassroots coalition building and a rejuvenation of extra-parliamentary politics. After its election, the Harris government wasted no time pursuing an aggressive anti-union agenda, as evidenced by the repeal of the NDP government's anti-scab law and reforms to the province's Labour Relations Act that made it more difficult to certify unions.[20] In response, organized labour and its community allies, temporarily disillusioned with party politics, sought to build union power by taking to the streets and exercising their democratic right to protest. The city-by-city demonstrations during the Harris government's first term were known as the "Days of Action," and the tagline for the St. Catharines event in May 1998 read, "Niagara Fights Back." In a flyer advertising the demonstration, event organizers wrote, "Our Premier has said 'he doesn't do protests.' He implies that there is another way to talk to this government. Those of us who have tried know better. Consultations held after announcements, 'town hall' meetings by invitation only, refusal after refusal of government members to meet with citizen groups — these actions are not democracy as we know it. When democracy is threatened, responsible citizens must protest." [21]

St. Catharines and District Labour Council president Ed Gould and Linda Rogers, a leader of the Niagara-based Golden Horseshoe Social Action Committee (GHSAC), acted as co-chairs for the event. After the defeat of the NDP government, many disillusioned left-wing activists in Niagara channelled their energy into groups like GHSAC, which formed a bridge between organized labour and social activists working in the peace movement, the environmental movement, and anti-poverty coalitions. In the days leading up to the St. Catharines march, the organizers commemorated workers who had died on the job as part of the annual Day of Mourning on 28 April. Community Awareness forums were held to discuss the impact of government cuts to social services, the arts, health care, and education, and a "tent city" and "jobs cemetery" were erected to shed light on the growing plight of the homeless and unemployed. [22]

On 1 May 1998, thousands of demonstrators from across Ontario gathered in the large parking lot below St. Paul Street in downtown St. Catharines and then marched throughout downtown streets, chanting, waving flags, and carrying placards denouncing the Harris government. The demonstrators eventually made their way to Montebello Park, in the heart of the city's downtown core, for a boisterous rally. [23] The Days of Action protests were significant in that they represented a shift in the way labour engaged in politics. Since the 1960s, the labour movement's political focus had been very much influenced by the political priorities of the NDP. However, the breakdown in party-union relations in the 1990s opened up a new world of possibilities for organized labour.

St. Catharines Day of Action, 1 May 1998.
Courtesy of the St. Catharines Museum (*St. Catharines Standard* Collection).

Despite the promise of independent political action in partnership with groups like GHSAC, most unions simply did not have the capacity to develop a culture of political action outside the scope of electoral politics. By the time the 1999 Ontario election rolled around, most union leaders were solidly behind the NDP once again and encouraged their members to forgive and forget. Some unions, however, opted not to return to the NDP fold.[24]

In August 2006, CAW convention delegates voted to sever all ties to the NDP after their president, Buzz Hargrove, was kicked out of the party for promoting a strategic voting scheme in the 2006 federal election that called on voters in some ridings to cast ballots for Liberal candidates in an effort to prevent a Conservative victory.[25] Adopting strategic voting was not new: several unions (including teachers, nurses, and building and construction trades) had adopted the same tactic in the 1999 Ontario election, in what proved to be an unsuccessful attempt to prevent the Mike Harris Conservatives from winning re-election. Hargrove's very public show of support for Prime Minister Paul Martin in 2006 was, however, the last straw for many New Democrats.

Hargrove's support for Martin did not sit well with local autoworkers in St. Catharines either. In fact, CAW Local 199 was one of the few autoworker locals that remained affiliated to the NDP despite the decision of the CAW convention. Local 199's loyalty to the NDP was, in part, explained by the personal political allegiances of the local union leadership, most of whom were committed NDP supporters.[26] Indeed, the local's president, Wayne Gates, had run as an NDP candidate in the Niagara Falls riding in the 2004 and 2006 federal elections, and the local's secretary-treasurer, Malcolm Allen, won a seat for the NDP in the Welland riding in the 2008 federal election. Allen was re-elected in 2011 as part of the NDP's electoral breakthrough, which saw the party form the official opposition in Ottawa for the first time in history.

Despite recent electoral successes, the politics of organized labour is certainly at a crossroads. While the labour-NDP relationship has yielded both benefits and occasional frustrations for workers in Niagara, history has demonstrated that, in the long run, unions need to take responsibility for their own futures by building the capacity of union members to defend their interests and promote their particular vision for society, independent of employers or politicians.

Welland MPP Peter Kormos (*back*) campaigns for federal NDP candidate Malcolm Allen (*front*) at a 2008 Labour Day demonstration in Niagara Falls. Courtesy of Marilyn Bellamy.

# Conclusion

Union stories of solidarity and struggle in Niagara stand as an example for many other places in Canada. The growth and development of labour unions as a political and economic force, in Niagara and elsewhere in the country, have delivered benefits to the working class that otherwise would have been unrealizable. In the workplace, unions have managed to win wage increases, basic employment standards, occupational health and safety laws, and better working conditions.

Beyond the workplace, by actively promoting human rights, affordable housing, and universal public health care, organized labour has been at the forefront of the larger struggle for social justice and economic equality. Thanks in part to the participation of women and immigrants in unions, the labour movement in Niagara has grown more responsive to the needs and interests of a wider cross-section of working people. Since World War II, here and elsewhere, unions have played a key role in making racial discrimination unlawful. In increasing numbers, women now serve on union and labour council executives, and not merely as recording secretaries.

At the same time, new market realities in the Niagara region, as elsewhere in Canada, present serious challenges to the labour movement. As we have seen, massive plant closures, the increasing replacement of steady, well-paying, unionized blue-collar jobs with ill-paid, part-time, non-unionized casual and contractual work, primarily in the service sector, have led to a decline in the size and strength of private sector unions. In Niagara's agricultural industry, the replacement of immigrant workers with migrant workers from the Caribbean and Latin America, under a program that prevents them from settling in Canada, presents additional challenges to the labour movement. In these circumstances, labour unions are among the few remaining defences against the pressures of neoliberal globalization, which consistently favours corporate power and profit and environmental expediency over the health and well-being of workers and their families.

That said, there is nothing inevitable about the resurgence of working-class power. History has demonstrated that political and economic elites will never voluntarily acquiesce to union demands for dignity, respect, and fairness in the workplace. Only through confrontation and struggle have workers witnessed political, economic, and social transformations that ultimately benefitted working-class people and their communities. Niagara's labour movement can rightly take pride in its long history of building union power, celebrate decades of united effort in the interest of working people, and draw inspiration from its past struggles and successes. But it must also prepare for the many challenges and transformations that lie ahead.

# Notes

## Canallers Fight for Work and Fair Wages

1 For a comprehensive study of workers on North American canals, see Peter Way, *Common Labour: Workers and the Digging of North American Canals, 1780–1860* (Cambridge and New York: Cambridge University Press, 1993).

2 Ruth Bleasdale, "Class Conflict on the Canals of Upper Canada in the 1840s," in *Pre-Industrial Canada, 1760–1849*, ed. Michael S. Cross and Gregory S. Kealey (Toronto: McClelland and Stewart, 1985), 103.

3 Ibid., 114.

4 *St. Catharines Journal*, 7 July 1842, quoted in Bleasdale, "Class Conflict," 111.

5 Way, *Common Labour*, 246–48.

## The Early Labour Movement

1 *Report of the Royal Commission on the Relations of Capital and Labor in Canada*, vol. 6, *Evidence, Ontario* (Ottawa: A. Senecal, 1889; CIHM/ ICMH Digital Series no. 9-08114), testimony of Robert James Mills, cigar maker, 919–22.

2 Ibid., testimony of J. R. Pettitt, Grimsby, 849; testimony of B. R. Nelles, Grimsby, 890–91.

3 Ruth A. Frager and Carmela Patrias, *Discounted Labour: Women Workers in Canada, 1870–1939* (Toronto: University of Toronto Press, 2005), 17–53.

4 Karen Dubinsky, "'The Modern Chivalry': Women and Labour in Ontario, 1880–1891," MA thesis, Carleton University, 1985; Gregory S. Kealey and Bryan D. Palmer, *Dreaming of What Might Be: The Knights of Labor in Ontario* (Toronto: New Hogtown Press, 1987), 321–26.

5   Kealey and Palmer, *Dreaming of What Might Be*, 105, 150–51; David Goutor, *Guarding the Gates: The Canadian Labour Movement and Immigration, 1872–1934* (Vancouver: University of British Columbia Press, 2007), part 2.

6   Kealey and Palmer, *Dreaming of What Might Be*, 64, 85.

7   Ibid., 222, 241.

8   Ibid., 297.

9   Ibid., 356–57.

10  Ibid., 292.

11  Ibid., 371.

## Class and Ethnicity in the Early Twentieth Century

1   For a useful analysis of industrialization in the Niagara region, see John N. Jackson and Carole White, *The Industrial Structure of the Niagara Peninsula* (St. Catharines, ON: Department of Geography, Brock University, 1971).

2   Isabel Kaprielian-Churchill, *Like Our Mountains: A History of Armenians in Canada* (Montreal and Kingston: McGill-Queens University Press, 2005), 243, 253. See also Pamela Sugiman, "Privilege and Oppression: The Configuration of Race, Gender and Class in Southern Ontario Auto Plants, 1939–1949," *Labour/Le Travail* 47 (Spring 2001): 83–113.

3   On calculations concerning the costs of labour turnover, see Harvard Business School, Baker Library, Plymouth Cordage Company Collection (hereafter PCC), H-4, topical files: Manufacturing Costs, Training, E. W. Brewster to Clark, 16 July 1920.

4   PCC, H-3, topical files: Industrial Relations, Welfare, General, *Employee Book of Information*, n.d., 6. See also Stuart D. Brandes, *American Welfare Capitalism, 1880–1940* (Chicago: University of Chicago Press, 1976).

5   *Welland Telegraph*, 30 November 1905.

6   Interview with Flavio Botari, Welland, October 1985.

7   Interview with Esch Orsini, Welland, October 1985.

8   Interview with Flavio Botari.

9   Interview with Elena Turroni, Welland, November 1985.

10  Brock University Library, Special Collections and Archives (hereafter BUL, Special Collections), Alfred Bolton and Barbara J. Austin, "'The Thorold Story': Pilkington in Canada," *Proceedings of the Administrative Science Association of Canada,* Business History Division, 1994.

11  BUL, Special Collections, Alfred Bolton, warehouse manager at Thorold, transcript of interview, Pilkington Group Archives and Records Service, Information Management and Storage, St. Helens, UK, 1944.

12  *Niagara Falls Daily Record,* 10 June 1916.

13  *Welland Tribune,* 28 March 1912.

14  *People's Press,* 30 May 1899, 6 June 1899, quoted in Fern A. Sayles, *Welland Workers Make History* (Welland, ON: By Winnifred Sayles, 1963), 116–17.

15 *Welland Telegraph,* 29 October and 12 November 1903.

16 Library and Archives Canada (hereafter LAC), RG 27, Department of Labour, vol. 98, file 424.01.7: Report of the Conference Held at St. Catharines, 8 September 1921, to Discuss Wages, Hours and Other Conditions on the Welland Canal.

17 For canallers' housing conditions, see LAC, RG 43, Department of Railways and Canals Fonds, Records Related to the Welland Canal (for example, vol. 2154, file 130; vol. 2156, file 258; vol. 2171, file 846).

18 *Niagara Falls Daily Record,* 24 June 1910.

19 Ibid.

20 *Niagara Falls Daily Record,* 25 June 1910.

21 LAC, RG 76, Immigration Branch, vol. 412, file 595173: Welland.

22 BUL, Special Collections, *Report on a Limited Survey of Relgious, Moral, Industrial and Housing Conditions Prepared for the St. Catharines Survey Committee by the Department of Social Service and Evangelism of the Methodist and Presbyterian Churches* (1915).

## Labour Revolt in Niagara

1 LAC, RG 43, Welland Canal, vol. 2917: Report by Lt. Col. Comp. 44th Reg., 11 November 1903; *People's Press,* 10 November 1903.

2 *Niagara Falls Daily Record,* 21 June 1910.

3 Archives of Ontario (hereafter AO), RG 18-76, *Records of the Commission to Enquire into and Report upon the Rates of Wages Paid to Men Employed by the Hydro-Electric Power Commission in the Construction of the Queenston-Chippawa Development, 1920* (hereafter *Queenston-Chippawa Development*), 90.

4 AO, RG 4-32, Attorney General's Department, file 1921, no. 165: Frank Collins, Chief of Police, to W. E. Raney, Attorney General, 14 January 1921; LAC, Arthur Lewis Sifton Papers, MG 27, II D19, vol. 9, Notes of the work of the C.I.B. Division for the week of 4 November 1920, 18. We are grateful to Jim Naylor for bringing the reference in the Sifton papers to our attention.

5 *Welland Telegraph,* 12 November 1903.

6 AO, RG 4-32, file 1908, no. 1707: L. H. Cole, District Trades and Labor Council, St. Catharines to Attorney General of Ontario, 19 December 1908.

7 *Industrial Banner,* 12 May and 19 May 1916; James Naylor, *The New Democracy: Challenging the Social Order in Industrial Ontario, 1914–1925* (Toronto: University of Toronto Press, 1991), 62.

8 *Welland Tribune,* 5 June 1918.

9 Naylor, *New Democracy,* 127.

10 Ibid., 148–49.

11 *Queenston-Chippawa Development,* 134.

12   Ibid., 175.

13   Ibid.

14   *Queenston-Chippawa Development,* Preliminary Report, 3–4, observations of Mr. MacBride.

15   Ibid., 1.

16   Ibid., 2–3.

17   *Niagara Falls Evening Review,* 17 May 1920. See also Naylor, *New Democracy,* 231

18   Naylor, *New Democracy,* 210.

19   AO, RG 23-26, OPP Criminal Investigations Records, file 93/6: Strikes, 1921, Depositions and Affidavits concerning the Beaver Board strike.

20   Ibid.

21   *Welland Telegraph,* 11 December 1917.

22   *People's Press,* 27 November 1917.

23   *Welland Telegraph,* 11 December 1917.

24   Ibid.

## Welfare Capitalism in Niagara

1    PCC, H-3, topical files: Industrial Relations, Welfare, General, B. Preston Clark, Chairman, Industrial Homes and Gardens, n.d.

2    PCC, H-3, topical files: Industrial Relations, Labor, "The Present Unrest," speech by Mr. Clark, 1913.

3    S. E. Morrison, *The Ropemakers of Plymouth: A History of the Plymouth Cordage Company, 1824–1949* (Boston: Houghton Mifflin, 1950), 94.

4    PCC, H-3, topical files: Industrial Relations, Welfare, Social Work, R. W. Brown, Supt., 5 April 1922.

5    Interview with "M.T.," Welland, November 1985.

6    PCC, Mr. Brewster's Files, O-6: Labor, Report by P. W. Viets (Head of Department of Industrial Relations, 1927–37), n.d.

7    PCC, H-3, topical files: Industrial Relations, Mr Marshall's Reports, C. P. Marshall to Mr. Holmes, n.d.

8    PCC, H-3, topical files: Industrial Relations, Labor, Welland Plant Council Records, F-38, memorandum, 13 April 1936.

9    PCC, PCC Council Records, F-31, minutes of the Inaugural Meeting, 10 August 1933; Welland Plant Council Records, F-37, 11 December 1934, statement of Mr. Holmes.

10   PCC, Mr. Brewster's Files, O-6: Labor, Employee Representation.

11   PCC, Welland Plant Council Records, F-37, 3 December 1935.

12   PCC, Welland Plant Council Records, F-37, 19 March 1937.

13   Interview with Mr. Triano, Welland, November 1985.

14   Interview with Esch Orsini, Welland, October 1985.

15   Interview with Flavio Botari, Welland, October 1985.

## Unemployment and Organization During the Great Depression

1  AO, RG 3-10, Premier Mitchell Hepburn Private Correspondence, box 265, file: Communism 1937, H. F. Logan, Barrister and Solicitor, Niagara Falls, to Mitchell Hepburn, 26 June 1937; AO, RG 23-26, OPP Criminal Investigations Records, Strike Files, file: 133-36, Re: Sam Krysman, Alleged Inflammatory Agitator, St. Catharines, Ont., 5 March 1937.

2  LAC, RG 27, Department of Labour, Strikes and Lockouts Files, vol. 366, Strike 21, 26 February 1934; vol. 393, Strike 334, 8 May 1936. See also *Kanadai Magyar Munkás*, 2 February 1937.

## The Crowland Relief Strike

1  AO, CP 2A 1210, Records of the Communist Party, National Executive Secretary of the W.U.L., to John Strush, Welland, 15 June 1931; CP 2A 1296, John Strush to A. Horvat, 20 July 1931; see also interview with John Strush, Hamilton, 1985; interview with Frank Haslam, Port Colborne, 1985.

2  Minutes, Crowland Township Council, 22 April 1933; *Welland Tribune*, 29 April 1933.

3  *Welland Tribune*, 12 December and 20 December 1934, 2 January and 5 January 1935.

4  *Welland Tribune*, 1 April 1935.

5  *Welland Tribune*, 9 April 1935.

6  *Welland Tribune*, 11 April 1935.

7  *Toronto Daily Star*, 26 April 1935.

8  *Welland Tribune*, 13 April 1935.

9  *Toronto Globe*, 30 April 1935.

10  AO, RG 4, Department of Attorney General, series 4-23, Criminal and Civil Files, 1935, 1222, T. D. Cowper, Country Crown Attorney, Welland, to I. A. Humphries, Department of Attorney General, 7 May 1935.

11  AO, RG 3, Hepburn Papers, General Correspondence, Box 192, Crowland Jobless, Thomas Martin to Mitchell Hepburn, 19 May 1935.

12  *Welland Tribune*, 11 May 1935.

## The Cotton Mill Strike, 1936–37

1  LAC, RG 27, Department of Labour, Strikes and Lockouts Files, vol. 380, Strike 196, Report from Manager, Empire Cotton Mills, to Department of Labour, Canada, 28 December 1936.

2  AO, RG 7-1-0-143, Department of Labour, Geo. G. Halcrow, District Inspector, Department of Labour, to Jos. R. Prain, Chief Inspector of Labour, Ontario, 30 January 1936.

3  Interview with Ida Farioli, Welland, November 1986, and interview with Martha Bertothy, Welland, November 1986.

4  *Welland Tribune*, 8 January 1937.

5  *Welland Tribune*, 2 January 1937.

6  *Welland Tribune*, 30 December 1936.
7  *Welland Tribune*, 22 December 1936.
8  *Welland Tribune*, 12 January 1937.
9  *Globe and Mail*, 21 January 1937.
10 *Toronto Clarion*, 14 January 1936.
11 *Kanadai Magyar Munkás*, 7 January 1937.
12 *Daily Clarion*, 2 January 1937.
13 *Welland Tribune*, 19 January 1937.
14 *Welland Tribune*, 17 January 1937.
15 AO, RG 7-1-0-143, Department of Labour, O. C. Jennette, Department of Labor, Industrial Standard Branch, to J. F. Marsh, Deputy Minister of Labour, 4 January 1937.
16 AO, RG 7-1-0-143, Department of Labour, L. B. Spencer to David A. Croll, 6 January 1937.
17 *Toronto Telegram*, 31 December 1936.
18 AO, RG 7-1-0-143, Department of Labour, E. J. Anderson, M.P.P., to Arthur B. Damude, M.P., 26 January 1937.
19 AO, RG 7-1-0-143, Department of Labour, Geo. G. Halcrow, District Inspector, Department of Labour, Ontario, to Jos. R. Prain, Chief Inspector of Labour, 30 January 1936.
20 *Welland Tribune*, 9 January 1937.
21 Interview with Father László Forgách, Toronto, August 1978.
22 AO, RG 7-1-0-143, Department of Labour, O. C. Jennette, Department of Labor, Industrial Standard Branch, to David A. Croll, Minister of Labour, 26 January 1937.
23 *Welland Tribune*, 17 February 1936.
24 Interview with Father László Forgách.

## The Monarch Strike

1  See *Report of the Royal Commission on the Textile Industry* (Ottawa: King's Printer, 1938). See also LAC, RG 33, series 20, vol. 19, Royal Commission on Textile Industry, Transcript of Hearings, vol. 5, 8 October 1936, Dunnville, Ontario, 9137.
2  LAC, RG 33, series 20, vol. 19, Royal Commission on the Textile Industry, Transcript of Hearings, vol. 5, 8 October 1936, Dunville, Ontario, 9209 ff.
3  AO, RG 7-30-0-48, Department of Labour, Strike, Monarch Knitting Co. Ltd., St. Catharines, 1938.
4  LAC, RG 33, series 20, vol. 51, Royal Commission on Textile Industry, Wage Questionnaires, Monarch Knitting Co. Ltd., St Catharines.

## The CIO at McKinnon Industries

1  Isabel Kaprielian-Churchill, *Like Our Mountains: A History of Armenians in Canada*, 245.

2   AO, RG 23-26, OPP Criminal Investigations Records, Strike Files, McKinnon Industries and General Motors Workers, St. Catharines, Attempts at agitation by Sam Krysman, file: 133-6, Re: Sam Krysman, Alleged Inflammatory Agitator, St. Catharines, Ont., 5 March 1937.

3   *St. Catharines Standard*, 6 March 1937.

4   Quoted in Kaprielian-Churchill, *Like Our Mountains*, 258.

5   *The Oshawa Labor Press*, 25 August 1938.

## Fighting for Democracy on the Home Front, 1939–45

1   AO, Select Committee to Inquire into Collective Bargaining Between Employers and Employees, RG 49-116, vol. 11, 16 March 1943, submission of St. Catharines Citizens' Delegation, 1263.

2   *Niagara Falls Evening Review*, 20 September 1941.

3   *St. Catharines Standard*, 23 September 1941.

4   Ibid.

5   *St. Catharines Standard*, 27 September 1941.

6   *St. Catharines Standard*, 13 September 1941.

7   *St. Catharines Standard*, 11 September, 12 September, and 19 September 1941.

8   Doug Smith, *Cold Warrior: C. S. Jackson and the United Electrical Workers* (St. John's: Canadian Committee on Labour History, 1997), 118.

9   Interview with Mike Bosnich, Welland, 11 November 1985.

10  AO, RG 7-30-217, b354934, Industrial Disputes Inquiry, Atlas Steels, J. P. Nicol, Industrial Disputes Inquiry Commissioner, to M. M. Maclean, Director of Industrial Relations and Registrar, Department of Labour, Ottawa, Re: Atlas Steels Limited, Welland, Ontario, and Re: Vote of employees, 18 June 1943 and 22 June 1943; RG 7-60, Department of Labour Applications for Certification, 1943-44, box 270767, file 12, UE vs. Atlas Steels. See also Smith, *Cold Warrior*, 119.

11  *Niagara Falls Evening Review*, 28 October 1943.

12  AO, RG 49-116, Records of the Selective Committee to Inquire into Collective Bargaining Between Employers and Employees, vol. 8, 708, Petition from Citizens of the Niagara Peninsula.

13  *Niagara Falls Evening Review*, 17 September 1941.

14  *Niagara Falls Evening Review*, 15 September and 17 September 1941.

15  LAC, MG 28, I 190, United Electrical, Radio and Machine Workers of America, vol. 1, file 6, UE District 5 Council 21st Annual Convention, 31 October–3 November 1957, UE pamphlets.

16  Interview with Harry Kurahara, quoted in Addie Kobayashi, *Exiles in Our Own Country: Japanese Canadians in Niagara* (Richmond Hill, ON: Nikkei Network of Niagara, 1998), 92.

17  *St. Catharines Standard*, 17 April 1940 and 27 September 1941.

18  AO, Select Committee to Inquire into Collective Bargaining Between Employers and Employees, RG 49-116, vol. 11, 16 March 1943.

### Niagara Labour's Cold War

1  LAC, MG 31, B 19, Madeleine Parent and R. Kent Rowley fonds, Local Union Files, vol. 2, file 14: Local 174, Plymouth Cordage Limited, Welland, Ontario, Correspondence 1947, 1949; vol. 12, file 8, Local 174, Plymouth Cordage Company, Welland, Ontario, Correspondence, O.L.R.B. Reports, Seniority Lists, Union Membership Lists and Notes, 1947–49; AO, RG 7-30-0-927, Conciliation, Mediation and Arbitration files, Plymouth Cordage Co., Welland, 1948. See also Fern A. Sayles, *Welland Workers Make History*, 170–71.

2  *Niagara Falls Evening Review*, 28 October 1943.

3  *Niagara Falls Evening Review*, 14 July and 29 July 1953.

4  *Niagara Falls Evening Review*, 18 August 1953.

5  LAC, MG 28, I 190, United Electrical, Radio and Machine Workers of America, vol. 24, files 5–7: English Electric Company of Canada Ltd., St. Catharines, Ont., Material issued to English Electric and Packard Electric, 1944–50; files 9–10: English Electric Company of Canada Ltd., St. Catharines, Ont., Materials and correspondence re: J. Bacon and Group, 1948.

### Women and Workers of Colour in the 1950s and 1960s

1  *St Catharines Standard*, 10 September 1959.

2  Ibid.

3  *St. Catharines Standard*, 11 September 1959.

4  *Toronto Telegram*, 11 September 1959.

5  LAC, MG 28, V75, Records of the Jewish Labour Committee of Canada, vol. 42, file 15, Correspondence, Reports, September–October 1959.

6  *Toronto Telegram*, 11 September 1959.

7  *St. Catharines Standard*, 11 September 1959.

8  *St. Catharines Standard*, 15 September 1959.

9  *Sydney Cape Breton Post*, 16 September 1959.

10  *St. Catharines Standard*, 26 October and 27 October 1959.

11  *St. Catharines Standard*, 15 September 1959.

12  *St. Catharines Standard*, 22 March 1960.

13  For the role of the St. Catharines and District Labour Council and the Toronto and District Labour Committee for Human Rights, see BUL, Special Collections, St. Catharines and District Labour Council files, general correspondence, 1957–63; LAC, MG 28, V75, Records of the Jewish Labour Committee of Canada, vol. 23, Circulars and Clippings, "Submissions re: racial discrimination in apartment buildings and multiple dwelling units"; vol. 42, file 15: Correspondence and Reports, September–October 1959; file 16: Correspondence and Reports, November–December 1959.

14  *St. Catharines Standard*, 3 May 1962.

15  Briefs of the Royal Commission on the Status of Women in Canada, Brief Presented to the Royal Commission on the Status of Women in Canada, Brief no. 8, 23 October 1967.

16  *St. Catharines Standard*, 6 June 1968.

## Ideologies Clashing: The 1970 UAW Strike

1  Confidential interview with union official, St. Catharines, September 2006.

2  Ibid.

3  *St. Catharines Standard*, 2 January 1971.

4  *St. Catharines Standard*, 17 December 1970.

5  *St. Catharines Standard*, 7 November 1970.

6  Ibid.

7  *St. Catharines Standard*, 18 December 1970.

8  *St. Catharines Standard*, 16 August 1982.

9  Confidential interview with union official, St. Catharines, September 2006.

10  Ibid.

11  Ibid.

12  Ibid.

## Strike Wave: 1972–76

1  Jon Peirce, *Canadian Industrial Relations*, 2nd ed. (Toronto: Prentice-Hall Canada, 2003), 344.

2  St. Catharines Public Library, "Niagara Peninsula — Strikes and Lockouts, 1968–1978," vertical file guide, Special Collections.

3  Ibid.

4  Leo Panitch and Donald Swartz, *From Consent to Coercion: The Attack on Trade Union Freedoms*, 3rd ed. (Aurora, ON: Garamond Press, 2003), 27.

5  Ibid., 32.

6  Ibid., 30.

7  *St. Catharines Standard*, 28 June 1975.

8  James McCrostie, *Just the Beginning! The Communications, Energy and Paperworkers Union of Canada* (Ottawa: Communications, Energy and Paperworkers Union of Canada, 1996), 17–18.

9  Allan Maslove and Gene Swimmer, *Wage Controls in Canada, 1975–78: A Study of Public Decision Making* (Montreal: Institute for Research on Public Policy, 1980), 148.

10  *St. Catharines Standard*, 14 October 1976.

11  *St. Catharines Standard*, 15 October 1976.

12  *St. Catharines Standard*, 20 January 1972.

13  BUL, Special Collections, St. Catharines and District Labour Council files, undated news clippings.

14  BUL, Special Collections, St. Catharines and District Labour Council files, correspondence from Kenneth Brisbois to Rudy Dick, 2 November 1972.

15  BUL, Special Collections, St. Catharines and District Labour Council files, correspondence from Rudy Dick to Kenneth Brisbois, 2 November 1972.

### Canadian Pulp and Paper Workers Fight Back

1  James McCrostie, *Just the Beginning! The Communications, Energy and Paperworkers Union of Canada*, 17.
2  Jamie Swift, *Walking the Union Walk: Stories from the Communications, Energy and Paperworkers Union* (Ottawa: Communications, Energy and Paperworkers Union of Canada, 2003), 63.
3  *St. Catharines Standard*, 2 September 1975.
4  *St. Catharines Standard*, 27 August 1975.
5  *St. Catharines Standard*, 6 September 1975.
6  *St. Catharines Standard*, 10 September 1975.
7  BUL, Special Collections, St. Catharines and District Labour Council files, meeting minutes, 1 October 1975.
8  BUL, Special Collections, St. Catharines and District Labour Council files, meeting minutes, 3 December 1975.

### Corporate Restructuring and Labour's Decline

1  *St. Catharines Standard*, 16 November 1981.
2  Ibid.
3  *St. Catharines Standard*, 17 June 1982.
4  Ibid.
5  *St. Catharines Standard*, 7 January 1983.
6  *St. Catharines Standard*, 6 April 1983.
7  Leo Panitch and Donald Swartz, *From Consent to Coercion: The Attack on Trade Union Freedoms*, 86.
8  Ibid., 96.

### The Eaton's Strike: Women Workers Walk the Line

1  *St. Catharines Standard*, 6 January 1985.
2  *St. Catharines Standard*, 4 February 1985.
3  *St. Catharines Standard*, 4 June 1985.
4  *St. Catharines Standard*, 4 February 1985.
5  *St. Catharines Standard*, 13 March 1985.
6  *St. Catharines Standard*, 15 April 1985.
7  BUL, Special Collections, St. Catharines and District Labour Council files, news clipping: Frances Phillips, "Eaton Dispute Stepped Up," n.d.
8  *St. Catharines Standard*, 14 May 1985.

## "Don't Lower the Standard": The Newsroom on Strike

1 Barbara Leiterman, "The Ascendancy of Conrad Black: Cost-cutting and Conservatism Are Trademarks of Canada's Media Mogul," *Extra!* November–December 1996, http://www.fair.org/index.php?page=1369.
2 *St. Catharines Standard*, 27 May 1998; BUL, Special Collections, St. Catharines and District Labour Council files, memo to affiliates, 23 May 1998.
3 Andrew Lundy, "CBC Lockout XVI: A View on the 'Strike Newspaper,'" *The Garret Tree*, 22 August 2005, http://robinrowland.com/garret/2005/08/cbc-lockout-xvi-view-on-strike.html.
4 *The Independent*, 30 May 1998.
5 Ibid.
6 *The Independent*, 13 June 1998.

## Occupation in Thorold

1 *Thorold News*, 23 October 1999.
2 Ibid.
3 Jamie Swift, *Walking the Union Walk: Stories from the Communications, Energy and Paperworkers Union*, 65.
4 *Globe and Mail*, 19 October 1999.
5 Swift, *Walking the Union Walk*, 65.
6 Ibid., 67.
7 Ibid., 65.

## Labour Builds Brock: Unions and the University

1 BUL, Special Collections, Brock University Founders' documents.
2 Ibid.
3 Ibid.
4 Ibid.
5 Edward Mitchelson "Labour and Brock Work Together," St. Catharines and District Labour Council, *Labour Review* (1968).
6 Interview with Lynn Williams, Toronto, 29 September 2006.
7 BUL, Special Collections, Brock University Founders' documents.
8 Interview with Lynn Williams.
9 BUL, Special Collections, Brock University Founders' documents.
10 Interview with Lynn Williams.
11 Ibid.
12 Lynn Williams, "The Labour Movement and the University," Larry Sefton Memorial Lecture, University of Toronto, 6 December 1982.
13 Jeffery Taylor, "Linking Labour Studies and Unions: Past Lessons and Future Visions," *Just Labour: A Journal of Work and Society* 4 (Spring 2004): 36.
14 Esther Reiter, "Labour Studies at Brock," St. Catharines and District Labour Council, *Labour Review* (1989): 23.

15   Canadian Association of University Teachers, "Brock Academic Staff Unionize," *CAUT Bulletin*, n.d., http://www.cautbulletin.ca/en_article. asp?articleid=2485.
16   Heidi Klose, "Here We Grow Again," *Education Forum* 28 (2002): 6–8.

## Living in a Dying Town: Deindustrialization in Welland

1    Canadian Labour Congress, *Communities in Crisis: Welland, Ontario* (2009), 10.
2    Ibid., 5.
3    *Toronto Star*, 3 September 2008.
4    Canadian Labour Congress, *Communities in Crisis*, 6.
5    Ibid., 5.
6    Confidential interview with union official, St. Catharines, January 2011.
7    *Welland Tribune*, 22 March 2009.
8    *Waterloo Record*, 28 November 2009.
9    *Welland Tribune*, 28 February 2010.
10   *Dear John: A Documentary* (2009), directed by Mark Lammert, One Three Four Films, Toronto.
11   *Toronto Star*, 3 September 2008.
12   Ibid.
13   *Welland Tribune*, 20 September 2008.
14   *Welland Tribune*, 26 February 2009.
15   Canada, *House of Commons Debates,* 40th Parliament, 1st Session, edited: *Hansard* no. 5, 24 November 2008. *Hansard* incorrectly quotes Allen as saying, "They told me they had thought they had finally found a secure job in an agri-region." But his words were "in the Niagara region."

## "Kicking Ass for the Working Class": Hotel Workers in Niagara

1    *Niagara Falls Review*, 28 April 1973.
2    Ibid.
3    *Niagara Falls Review*, 2 April 1993.
4    *Niagara Falls Review*, 27 August 1991.
5    Confidential interview with union official, St. Catharines, April 2011.
6    Ibid.
7    Ibid.
8    *Niagara Falls Review*, 23 December 1999.
9    *Niagara Falls Review*, 20 December 1999.
10   *Niagara Falls Review*, 24 December 1999.
11   Confidential interview with union official, St. Catharines, April 2011.
12   CTV News, "Ontario Unions Claim New Law Is 'Igniting a War,'" 2 November 2000, http://www.ctv.ca/CTVNews/TopStories/20001102/ctvnews77955/.
13   Confidential interview with union official, St. Catharines, April 2011.
14   *Niagara Falls Review*, 4 October 2002.

15  *Niagara Falls Review*, 22 November 2002.
16  *Niagara Falls Review*, 7 December 2002.
17  Confidential interview with union official, St. Catharines, April 2011.
18  *Niagara Falls Review*, 7 December 2002.
19  *Niagara Falls Review*, 9 December 2002.
20  Ibid.
21  Confidential interview with union official, St. Catharines, April 2011.
22  *Niagara Falls Review*, 16 December 2002.
23  *National Post*, 24 October 2007.
24  Ibid.
25  Confidential interview with union official, St. Catharines, April 2011.
26  UNITE HERE press release, 31 July 2007.
27  Ibid.
28  Confidential interview with union offical, St. Catharines, April 2011.
29  Ibid.
30  *Niagara Falls Review*, 1 September 2007.
31  *Niagara This Week*, 20 September 2006.
32  *Globe and Mail*, 9 December 2006.
33  *Niagara This Week*, 20 September 2006
34  *Globe and Mail*, 9 December 2006.
35  *St. Catharines Standard*, 13 December 2006.
36  UNITE HERE press release, 13 December 2006.
37  Ibid.
38  Ibid.
39  Ibid.
40  Confidential interview with union official, St. Catharines, April 2011.
41  UNITE HERE press release, 14 December 2006.
42  Michelle Hemmigson, speech to St. Catharines and District Labour Council, May 2007.
43  UNITE HERE press release, 16 June 2007.
44  Ibid.
45  Ibid.
46  Ibid.
47  UNITE HERE press release, 3 September 2007.
48  *Niagara Falls Review*, 3 September 2007.
49  Confidential interview with union official, St. Catharines, April 2011.
50  UNITE HERE press release, 17 October 2007.
51  *St. Catharines Standard*, 25 January 2008.
52  *Toronto Star*, 24 January 2008.
53  UNITE HERE press release, 24 January 2008.
54  *Niagara Falls Review*, 9 February 2008.
55  UNITE HERE press release, 8 February 2008.
56  Ibid.
57  Ibid.

58  Confidential interview with union official, St. Catharines, April 2011.
59  UNITE HERE press release, 15 December 2008.
60  *St Catharines Standard*, 5 February 2009.
61  *St. Catharines Standard*, 15 April 2009.
62  *St. Catharines Standard*, 7 April 2009.
63  Ibid.
64  *St. Catharines Standard*, 5 February 2009.
65  Confidential interview with union official, St. Catharines, April 2011.
66  UNITE HERE press release, 30 April 2008.
67  Workers United press release, 17 November 2010.

## The House Advantage: Organizing Niagara's Casinos

1   *Windsor Star*, 12 November 1994.
2   Ibid.
3   *Niagara Falls Review*, 3 November 1999.
4   Ontario Federation of Labour, "The OFL Action Plan: For a New Activism and a People's Charter," 5 December 2001, http://ofl.ca/uploads/library/policy_papers/TheOFLActionPlanAsAmended.pdf.
5   Ibid.
6   *Niagara Falls Review*, 18 January 2000.
7   *Niagara Falls Review*, 16 February 2000.
8   Buzz Hargrove, speech delivered at Brock University, 23 November 2009.
9   *Niagara Falls Review*, 1 May 2001.
10  *Niagara Falls Review*, 24 October 2001.
11  Confidential interview with union official, St. Catharines, April 2011.
12  *Niagara Falls Review*, 3 December 2003.
13  *Niagara Falls Review*, 8 December 2004.
14  *Niagara Falls Review*, 31 March 2005.
15  *Niagara Falls Review*, 23 November 2005.
16  Confidential interview with union official, St. Catharines, April 2011.
17  *Niagara Falls Review*, 2 May 2007.
18  Ibid.
19  UNITE HERE press release, 2 October 2007.
20  CAW press release, 22 January 2010.
21  CAW, "Where Are All the Full-Time GOOD Paying Jobs?" *The Real Deal*, n.d.
22  *Niagara Falls Review*, 2 February 2009.
23  Romel Argeta, speech delivered to the CAW Gaming Council, Niagara Falls, March 2010, http://www.youtube.com/watch?v=D-Y1docl2gs.
24  Niagara Casinos, "Casinos of Niagara — Make an Informed Decision!" n.d.
25  Ibid.
26  CAW, "Know the Facts Before You Vote!" n.d.
27  Ibid.
28  *Niagara Falls Review*, 21 April 2010.

29  *Niagara Falls Review*, 22 April 2010.
30  Confidential interview wih union official, St. Catharines, April 2011.
31  *Niagara Falls Review*, 18 May 2010.
32  Ibid.
33  *Niagara Falls Review*, 25 April 2010.
34  Confidential interview with union official, St. Catharines, April 2011.

## Migrant Farm Workers in Niagara

1  *Report of the Royal Commission on Price Spreads* (Ottawa: King's Printer, 1935), 67–72, 114–15, 153–57.
2  Addie Kobayashi, *Exiles in Our Own Country: Japanese Canadians in Niagara, passim*.
3  Vic Satzewich, *Racism and the Incorporation of Foreign Labour: Farm Labour Migration in Canada Since 1945* (London: Routledge, 1991).
4  AO, RG 16-102, Agricultural Manpower Services, b354994.
5  Kerry L. Preibisch, "Local Produce, Foreign Labor: Labor Mobility Programs and Global Trade Competitiveness in Canada," *Rural Sociology* 72, no. 3 (2007): 418–49.
6  *El Contrato* (2003), directed by Min Sook Lee, National Film Board of Canada, Montréal.
7  Sue Ferguson, "Hard Time in Canadian Fields: Conditions Can Be Tough for Our 19,000 Migrant Workers," *Maclean's*, 11 October 2004.
8  *Toronto Star*, 27 October 1994.
9  *Windsor Star*, 26 October 1994.
10  *Toronto Star*, 27 October 1994.
11  Petra Kukacka, "Agricultural Migrant Workers and the Struggle for Dignity: Mexican-Canadians Build Enlace Community Link," unpublished paper, 16 May 2005, home.oise.utoronto.ca/~lared/agricultural%20workeers.doc.
12  Agricultural Workers Alliance, "The Status of Migrant Farm Workers in Canada, 2010–2011," UFCW Canada, 2011.
13  Kate Andres-Toal, "Growing Respect for Offshore Workers," OPIRG-Brock. http://www.opirgbrock.org/node/75.
14  Agricultural Workers Alliance, "The Status of Migrant Farm Workers in Canada, 2010–2011."
15  Ibid.
16  Confidential interview with union official, St. Catharines, April 2011.
17  Agricultural Workers Alliance, "The Status of Migrant Farm Workers in Canada, 2010–2011."
18  Confidential interview with union official, St. Catharines, April 2011.
19  *Globe and Mail*, 29 April 2011.
20  *St. Catharines Standard*, 6 September 2011.
21  City of St. Catharines, "British Methodist Episcopal Church, Salem Chapel," http://www.stcatharines.ca/en/experiencein/BritishMethodist EpiscopalChurchSalemChapel.asp.

22  Justicia for Migrant Workers press release, 1 September 2011.
23  Justicia for Migrant Workers press release, 24 August 2011.
24  *St. Catharines Standard*, 6 September 2011.

**Organized Labour and the New Democratic Party in Niagara**

1  *St. Catharines Standard*, 2 June 1960.
2  Ibid.
3  *St. Catharines Standard*, 13 October 1967. See also Larry Savage, "We Know the Rotten Part of the Rich: Working-Class Politics in Thorold South" (BUL, Special Collections).
4  *Niagara Falls Review*, 1 March 2007; *Niagara This Week*, 2 March 2007.
5  Confidential interview with union official, St. Catharines, September 2006.
6  Thomas Walkom, *Rae Days: The Rise and Follies of the NDP* (Toronto: Key Porter Books, 1994), 239–40.
7  Leo Panitch and Donald Swartz, *From Consent to Coercion: The Attack on Trade Union Freedoms*, 178–80.
8  For further discussion, see Walkom, *Rae Days*; and George Ehring and Wayne Roberts, *Giving Away a Miracle* (Oakville, ON: Mosaic Press, 1993).
9  Walkom, *Rae Days*, 98–103.
10  Panitch and Swartz, *From Consent to Coercion*, 178–80.
11  *St. Catharines Standard*, 18 June 1993.
12  BUL, Special Collections, St. Catharines and District Labour Council files, *Hamilton Spectator*, n.d.
13  *St. Catharines Standard*, 4 June 1993.
14  BUL, Special Collections, St. Catharines and District Labour Council files, *Hamilton Spectator*, n.d.
15  Confidential interview with union official, St. Catharines, September 2006.
16  Walkom, *Rae Days*, 144.
17  Peter Kormos, "Betrayed: Social Contract Bill a Problem for All Working People," St. Catharines and District Labour Council, *Labour Review* (1993), 33–34.
18  Walkom, *Rae Days*, 121.
19  Ibid., 122.
20  Panitch and Swartz, *From Consent to Coercion*, 189–94.
21  BUL, Special Collections, St. Catharines and District Labour Council files, St. Catharines Day of Action Co-ordinating Committee, "The Ontario Way, the Niagara Way," n.d.
22  *St. Catharines Standard*, 22 April 1998.
23  *St. Catharines Standard*, 2 May 1998.
24  Larry Savage, "Contemporary Party-Union Relations in Canada," *Labor Studies Journal* 35, no. 1 (2010): 15.
25  Ibid.
26  Confidential interview with union official, St. Catharines, April 2011.

# Index

wage parity, 82–83

wages: and caps, 67; cut, 55; fair, 8–9, 30, 60; increase in, 70–73, 84, 89–91, 130, 133, 136, 143; living, 22, 156; low, 12–13, 25–27, 38–40, 47–53, 60, 150, 164; lower, 39, 45–46; minimum, 157, 166; negotiated, 61–63; and rent, 46; and women, 53, 60

Wagg, Virginia, 116

Walter Reuther Administration, 81–83

Washuta, John, 83

Welch, Alex, 46

welfare plan, 34–36, 38–39, 68

Welland and District Labour Council, 175

Welland Canal, 8–9, 14–17, 22, 28, 124, 189

Welland's *People's Press*, 21, 32

*Welland Telegraph*, 18, 22

White, John, 33

Williams, Lynn, 105–10

women, 74–84; and Empire Cotton Mills, 46; and gender inequality, 14; immigrant, 25, 164; married, 78, 80–81; and picket lines, 47; and politics, 175; self-supporting, 80; and service industry, 95; and supplemental wages, 13; and textile industry, 13, 45; and union support, 53, 56, 59; as unskilled workers, 12; and the vote, 29; and wage parity, 47; working-class, 13, 29; and World War II, 60, 68. *See also* workers, women

Woodcock, Leonard, 82

Woods, Jack, 74, 76

workers: Anglo-Canadian, 19–31; anti-union, 129; and Brock University, 105, 117; cafeteria, 117; canal, 8–10; cannery, 25; casino, 149–64; casino, unionized, 152, 155, 157; Chinese, 32; and class,

4, 16, 21, 36–37, 60; and class conflict, 34; clerical, 117; of colour, 74–81; and complaints, 54; and deindustrialization, 117–24; disabled, 15; and early manufacturing, 10–15; and ethnicity, 16–25; farm, 84, 167; health, 36, 70, 166; hotel, 124, 134, 147–48; injured, 124; Italian, 16, 18–22, 26–28, 34, 45–47; laundry, 145; and loneliness, 169; and loyalty, 18–19, 37, 152; maintenance, 88; migrant farm, 164–72; militant female, 60; minority, 56, 64; Native, 165; native-born, 22, 29; office, 19; part-time, 95, 97; postal, 3, 85; and protest, 25–34; public sector, 86, 142; racetrack, 161; rail, 21; restaurant, 132; seasonal, 24, 125, 164–65, 170; semi-skilled, 16; sheet metal, 85; shoe factory, 11; textile, 45, 51; tourism, 125, 145, 156; unorganized, 11, 28; unskilled, 10, 12–14, 28, 55; unskilled, as children, 12–13; and the welfare plan, 34–41; women, 14–15, 25, 65, 79–80, 95–98

Workers United, 148

workforce, 40, 114, 118, 123, 154–55, 163–64

work hours: canaller, 8, 30; and union, 11

workplace, 104, 114, 128, 131–33, 140, 147–54, 184–85; unionized, 67, 128

World War I, 25, 28–29, 34, 67

World War II: and employment discrimination, 32–33, 65; and labour shortages, 56; and profits, 57, 59; and war effort, 59–60, 67

Yale and Towne company, 71, 73